MOMENT OF MOMENTS

preparing for that
life-altering moment

Thirtysix.org

Moment of Moments

Preparing for that Life-Altering Moment

ISBN 9798653380976

Published by:
Thirtysix.org
22 Yitzchak Road
Telzstone, Kiryat Yearim
Israel   9083800

Time may **fly**,
but opportunity
vanishes when
overlooked.

PEOPLE WHO REACH their 90th birthday will have lived approximately 67 times 365 days plus 22 times 366 days, or 24,455 + 8,052 = 32,507 days. Multiply that sum by 24 hours per day, then by 60 minutes each hour, and finally by 60 seconds each minute, and the product becomes an incredible almost THREE TRILLION (2,808,604,800) seconds.

And yet an entire life can be MADE or BROKEN in any ONE of those moments. Although the moment itself can be years in the making, the life-altering moment itself will be but a step across a narrow threshold of time. The road to a decision may be long, but the actual decision, once made, is like the flick of a switch. You can call it the "moment of moments."

The Talmud says something similar here:

There are some who acquire their world after many years, and there are some who acquire their world in a SINGLE MOMENT. (Avodah Zarah 17a)

This is hard to comprehend. A moment of time can always be subdivided into ever smaller units of time AD INFINITUM, and in that respect it is INFINITE. Yet things happen. Changes occur. One moment a thing is something, and the next moment it is something else. Although the buildup to a change may take what seems like an eternity, there is a very SPECIFIC and EXACT moment—the THRESHOLD OF TIME— when something stops being what it previously was and in actuality becomes something new.

It may be impossible to calculate exactly when that moment will be, is, or was, but for humans that isn't necessary anyway. What IS necessary is to be READY for it whenever it does occur, and for THAT there is usually enough time for the person who cares.

The Talmud is basically saying this:

A person only sins when a spirit of insanity enters him. (Sotah 3a)

But are insane people responsible for their actions? If not, then why would they be culpable for their sins?

The answer is that they are not, at least not for the act of the sin per se. Starving people will have a difficult time sticking to their diets at a fancy wedding. Gabby people will have difficulty not speaking loshon hara among others who do. To quote the Talmud:

> This is comparable to a person who had a son, whom he bathed and anointed, fed and gave drink. Then he hung a purse around his neck and brought his son to the entrance of a brothel. What could the son do to avoid sinning? (Brochos 32a)

Not too much. By that time the son was a proverbial sitting duck for his yetzer hara. The father in the story handed his son over to the Satan on a silver platter, making him more a victim than a culprit, like everyone else who finds himself in too difficult a spiritual test. So again, why are such people deemed guilty of sin when they fail the test?

Because the Talmud is saying in both places that if you want to avoid sin, then you have to think ahead and avoid the things that lead to it. As it says:

> Who is a wise person? One who sees what is being born. (Tamid 32a)

The "wise person," the Talmud is saying, projects the current situation into the future, to be ready for it. If you want to stick to your diet at a feast, then don't go to it hungry. If you want to avoid speaking loshon hara, then stay away from people who speak it. If you want to avoid sin, then consider where and how it occurs, and avoid those places and situations as much as is reasonably possible.

In other words, it's not for the actual act of sin that people are punished if overcome by their yetzer haras at the moment of truth. They're guilty of the "sin" of not having anticipated the test and preparing for it in advance .

This can be made more clear by considering two passengers in a car, one in the front seat looking ahead and one in the back seat looking out the side window. The person looking ahead will see objects as they come toward the car and will be ready for them when they pass.

But the person in the back seat, who is looking out the side window, will only see the same objects when they disappear in a flash. Such people are never ready for the objects and may only realize what they really were after they vanish and can no longer be appreciated or dealt with. Life will be tense and perhaps frustrating.

The whole point of wisdom is to make us aware of important opportunities for getting the most out of life. In order to do that we have to first know what is important and then how to effectively go after it—and that takes a wise person.

Only people who do this can know how to look at the events of today and project them into the future for a potential impact on their lives. Everyone else will just drift through such events, remaining oblivious of their potential for good or bad until well after the time it is possible to harness the good or avoid the bad.

Life is made up of an INCREDIBLE number of decisions, but only a handful—perhaps even just one—can determine the ENTIRE fate of a person both in THIS world AND the next one. People have either lived or died because of a single decision which FOR-EVER changes their lives and often the lives of others as well.

But we know this already. So many times we have really wanted something and knew that getting it could come down to a single thing we said or did. We are sometimes aware that a critical moment of success or failure is approaching, and that how we respond can determine something one way or the other. Stories have been told, books have been written, and movies have been made about countless momentous mo-ments.

But those were the obvious ones, mostly because they occurred in the past, and retroactively we could figure out what caused them and what went right or wrong. Far more have gone undetected because we are not clear what they were or how they may have caused a good or bad outcome. Since we didn't know about them in advance, we weren't ready for them when they came, and didn't even know that they had already passed.

And then there are those yet to come, and in particular, one MAJOR future moment. The unnerving thing about this is that it may actually be happening already or, even worse, may have already occurred. Either consciously or unconsciously we made a choice that determined whether or not we will survive the Messianic Era and beyond.

For years now we have been making decisions that determined our outlook on life and history, and THESE decisions are shaping our future today. They are the lens through which we examine the events occurring in our life and which direct our response to them. Is God involved? Is He not involved? Are these messianic times? Are they not messianic times?

It is important to point out, therefore, that if we have previously decided incorrectly, we will continue to decide incorrectly, no matter how much we think we are deciding correctly…no matter how confident we may be in our decision-making ability. So when THE moment of truth finally arrives, and it WILL, now sooner than later, we'll either run to it or be run over by it. Which it will be depends on how correctly we have decided until now…in advance of that moment.

But how can we know?
That's what this book is about.

The First Thing To Know…
one

WHAT IS THE purpose of life? This question is simple to ask but a killer to answer. There are almost as many opinions and variations as there are people in the world, and that's over 7.8 billion people. How could something so FUNDAMENTAL to a meaningful life be SO misunderstood?

That is simple.

It goes back to the Chet Aitz HaDa'as Tov v'Ra, the sin of eating from the Tree of Knowledge of Good and Evil.[1] Physical death wasn't the only consequence of that historic faux pas. Intellectual clarity also died that day, and man has grappled with the truth about life ever since.

---

[1] Bereishis 3:1.

Had that been the only issue, however, we would probably still have been better off than we were and are. Then we could at least find the will to turn to God, beg for forgiveness, and perhaps plead for help to correctly work life out.

But there is the issue of the yetzer hara, usually translated as the "evil inclination," the effects of which are best described by this:

> After Rabbi Alexandri prayed, he would say the following: "Master of the Universe, it is revealed and known before You that our will is to perform Your will, but what prevents us? The 'yeast in the dough…'" (Brochos 17a)

It is the yeast in the dough, aka the yetzer hara, that prevents people from doing what they REALLY want to do: serve God…pursue truth…live meaningful lives, etc. We'd like to go to the right, but the yetzer hara drives us left:

> A person has two kidneys; one advises him to [do] good and to do evil. It stands to reason [that the one advising him to do] good is to his right and [the one that advises him to do] evil is to his left, as it says: "A wise man's understanding is at his right hand, but a fool's understanding is at his left" (Koheles 10:2). (Brochos 61a)

One person, two very opposite sides. There is the ESSENCE of the person, the SOUL—which only wants to do right by God.[2] And then there is the yetzer hara—which is not actually the person himself but rather an add-in as a consequence of the first man's sin—which often acts as if it owns the place.[3] If doing the will of God in any way interferes with its physical enjoyment of this world, it will push in the opposite direction.

The result can only be INTERNAL psychological warfare.[4] But all wars get tiring after a while, and this one usually ends up creating a proverbial fork in the ideological road.

To go to the right requires a life in pursuit of the necessary means to not only defend against the yetzer hara, but to put it behind bars—in order to stay safe from it. Going to the left means capitulation to its approach to life, however despicable it might make the person.

History has been about the choice billions of people have made between the two, with the clear emphasis on the choice of capitulation. True, it does not always have to be one or the other—the level of capitulation can vary both from person to person and

---

[2] Sha'ar HaGilgulim, Introduction 1, and countless other sources written before and after it.
[3] Sha'ar HaGilgulim, Introduction 23.
[4] The Way of God, Part 1, Ch. 2:1.

from time to time. But equally clear is how few have taken the time and expended the energy to subdue and harness the yetzer hara. Proportionally it's as if they almost haven't existed.

The yetzer hara is like a lion.[5] It eats people instinctively. But capture and secure it behind bars, and it will merely yawn and peacefully go to sleep on its paws if it sees someone on the other side of the cage. If anything, a person is simply an annoyance.

But should the bars happen to go up while someone is standing there, the lion will suddenly awaken. Instead of yawning, it will lick its chops as the idea of dinner runs through its mind and the person immediately runs for protection. Someone who does not find it will be eaten alive.[6]

In the analogy the visitor is the person's soul, temporarily housed in the body. The lion of course is the yetzer hara, which is truly like a hungry lion:

> Sin crouches at the door, and to you is its desire. (Bereishis 4:7)

> Rebi Shimon ben Levi says: "A person's inclination overpowers him every day, and seeks to kill him… (Kiddushin 30b)

---

[5] See Yoma 69b.

[6] See Succah 52b.

Unrestrained, the lion within us all instinctively can result in this:

> It is taught in the name of Rebi Meir: Why was the Torah given to the Jewish people? Because they are arrogant…and had Torah not been given to the Jewish people, no nation or tongue could withstand them. (Beitzah 25b)

And the bars of the cage? Are they keeping us safe in everyday life? What are they?

CLARITY about the purpose of life:

> The Holy One, Blessed Is He, said to the Jewish people: "My children, I created the evil inclination and I created Torah as its antidote. If you are engaged in Torah you will not be given over into its hand…" (Kiddushin 30b)

> The school of Rabbi Yishmael taught: "My son, if this wretched one encounters you, pull it into the study hall…" (Kiddushin 30b)

You see it in the secular world all the time. College students who remember why they came in the first place will sacrifice fun to study, pass exams, and graduate. Business people will give up things they enjoy most in order to close a deal that will change their careers. Couples will forego a trip or new car to save for their dream house. When people are clear about what they want, they have the strength to fight off distraction from it.

Life, however, is not a temporary college course or a career to build a better lifestyle. It is certainly much bigger than a new house. But life is also quite automatic, something you can't really opt into or out of. That makes it easier to just go along for the ride, if you're one of the fortunate who have at least managed to survive.

There's another problem. If you want to know the requirements for graduation from school, you know where to find them. If you need help, you know how to get it. Ditto for the business world. When it comes to MAN-MADE systems, in order to succeed with them you need to know how they work, and there are ways to find out.

That's not true of life though. Even atheists agree that man had nothing to with his own creation, and most of what we have learned about ourself has been on the job. Where can you go to find out how man was made, ALL of him, not just his body? Who can you ask about the definition of success and failure, and how to achieve the former while avoiding the latter?

Enter the controversy. Every religion has claimed that right and honor, and each has developed its own way of life based on its belief. This has only served to further muddy an already muddled issue, leaving different people going in direction life-directions—and each assumes he has it right and everyone else has it wrong.

It has left a lot of people in intellectual limbo, especially now that science has greatly increased its stake at the table. Science has greatly demystified the natural world, and religions that depended on such mysteries to keep them going are dying. Or the adherents just turn their backs on all other sources of knowledge but their own, and maintain blind faith.

They all make preposterous claims, as does science. But one of them makes the most preposterous claim of all: Torah Judaism states emphatically that it was not only received directly from God Himself by the ENTIRE nation of 3,000,000 people, but every word of the Written Law was dictated by Him to Moshe Rabbeinu, letter by letter, word by word.

And have you seen what's inside? It is fantastically detailed, elaborate, and interconnected. There has been nothing really like it until recent times when a massive body of information can be gathered from the internet and libraries. It has also accumulated over thousands of years, and as of late has had the benefit of modern science and technology to compile and record it!

The Torah, on the other hand, has been just as it is now for thousands of years, long before man was smart enough and had enough know-how to create it. And that's before even going into the secrets of Kabbalah, the understanding of which goes farther than modern science with its own limitations can ever go.

But this is not a proof-of-Torah book. It is rather a buildup to the idea that if any body of knowledge or way of thinking has the best credentials to at least propose to know the most about life, it is Torah. Other belief systems may talk more to some people than others, but that is because they are talking to a partnership of body and soul in which the body may still have too much of a say.

There is plenty of room for the yetzer hara in a Torah home as well, and in some cases even more. But that only applies when people do not take the time to apply the teachings of Torah well enough to keep the bars between the "lion" and themselves intact.

Having said that, it is time to see what Torah says about man, his mission, and where he needs to be.

What In The World Is Man?

two

WHAT IN THE world is man? This is actually two questions and both are important: What is man and what is man's role in the world?

There are different ways to answer the first question, but the most instructive one is the kabbalistic description. Man is a medabehr–speaker, the highest of four levels of created elements, although he has aspects of each of the lower three levels in him as well. The levels are Domaim–Silent, Tzomayach–Vegetation, Chayah–Living, and Medabehr–Speaker.[1]

Linguists may be some of the very few who appreciate the value of language and how it distinguishes mankind from all other living beings. But even they

---

[1] Sha'ar HaGilgulim, Introduction 29.

overlook its ultimate importance to man and history, beginning with this verse and explanation:

> God formed man from dust of the ground and breathed into his nostrils a living soul, and the man became a living spirit. (Bereishis 2:7)

> A living spirit: a speaking spirit. (Onkeles)

You would not know it from that way most people speak, but speech is a function of the essence of a person, his soul. If speech isn't holy, then it has been hijacked by the yetzer hara. The Zohar says:

> From a man's mouth you can tell what he is. (Zohar, Balak 193b)

Is it a coincidence therefore that the more spiritually sophisticated a person becomes, the more refined his speech becomes? Not in light of these insights:

> Rebi Elazar said: "Every man was created to toil, as it says, 'Because man was made to toil' (Iyov 5:7). I do not know if that means to toil through speech or actual labor. However, when it says, 'A toiling soul toils for him, for his mouth compels him' (Mishlei 16:26), I know that a person was created to toil with his mouth. I do not know though

if this means to toil in Torah or just in mundane conversation. But when it says, 'This Torah should not leave your mouth' (Yehoshua 1: 8), I know that man was created to toil in Torah [speech]." (Sanhedrin 99b)

Rava said: Anyone who speaks of unholy matters (Rashi: childishly) has transgressed a positive commandment, as it says, "Speak of them" (Devarim 6:7): them (Rashi: words of Torah) and not other words. (Yoma 19b)

Anyone who speaks distastefully will cause a negative decree from heaven, even if he has 70 years of merits in his favor. (Kesuvos 8b)

The Holy One, Blessed Is He, only made a covenant with the Jewish people because of the oral things (i.e., the Oral Law), as it says, "For it is according to these words that I have made a covenant with you and with the Jewish people" (Shemos 34: 27). (Gittin 60b)

There are many points to explain here and many questions to answer. But one thing is clear from the start: talk is NOT cheap. On the contrary, people may be accumulating a word debt greater than they'll ever be able to afford to pay!

And don't be fooled by the expression that "actions speak louder than words." That's only true when someone is trying to earn the trust of fellow human beings who can only tell what you think from what you do. THEY need the act as a confirmation of the word.

But as constructive or destructive as actions can be, words are even more so. Even God Himself spoke Creation into existence. And just because we can't always see what our words build or destroy doesn't mean that they haven't done so. Won't we be surprised, perhaps even shocked, when we see later in history just what our words created or, God forbid, destroyed.

But speech is just the beginning of the story, or actually, the middle of it. Words are the result of something else, like tools in the hand of a craftsman. The tools have the potential to accomplish all kinds of incredible things, but only as a function of the will of the person holding them.

Likewise, words are merely organized phonetic sounds, arranged in such a way as to create a common basis for the communication of ideas. But their meaning is defined completely by the person using them, by what is intended to be conveyed by them. If someone making a statement intends to express something but carelessly uses words incorrectly, even a statement that sounds offensive might not have that intention at all, and the person making the statement might not even have a chance to explain himself before great damage is done.

Thus if people need to make a speech that might have great impact on their future, they will take the time and expend the energy to thoughtfully construct it. It will be far from casual, with just about every word being handpicked for its ability to accurately and appropriately convey the intended message. It will be in the end a veritable literary work of art.

Just as a person's face is a way to see what is going on inside the person, words tell what and how we are thinking. Lucid speech means lucid thought. Unintelligible speech means random thinking. Words are the clothing of our thoughts, which is why "when wine goes in, secrets go out."[2]

Perhaps Onkeles' statement that a living spirit is a speaking spirit should be emended to a "thinking" spirit. Why only speech? It must be a combination of both: man is a COMMUNICATOR OF THOUGHTS. We're not here just to think. We're here to communicate what we think.

Anything we think? Clearly not, as it says:

And God said, "Let us make man in our image, after our likeness…" (Bereishis 1:26)

---

2 Eiruvin 65a.

If we were made b'tzelem Elokim—in the image of God—shouldn't we act like it? The Torah will later advise us:

> This day I call on the heaven and the earth as witnesses [that I have warned] you: I have set before you life and death, the blessing and the curse. Choose life, so that you and your offspring will live." (Devarim 30:19)

In the end, man is not just a speaking spirit, and he is not only a communicator of ideas. He is meant to be a COMMUNICATOR OF GODLY IDEAS. That describes who we are and what we are meant to be doing in this world. How are we doing so far?

To be clear, even the most mundane idea can be godly if it is used in a godly way. When someone said, "Hey, pass me that brick" to build Migdal Bavel,[3] it was profane speech. When someone said the exact same thing to build the Temple, it was holy speech. Hence God condemns the former by saying:

> And God said, "[They are] one people, and they all have one language, and this is what they have decided to do?" (Bereishis 11:6)

---

[3] Tower of Babel.

So what did God specifically do in response? He said to His Heavenly Tribunal:

> Come, let us descend and confuse their language, so that one will not understand the language of his companion. (Bereishis 11:7)

Powerful. Who would have thought that in such an action-oriented world, even called by Kabbalah *Olam Asiyah*—World of Action—that speech would be at the center of it all? Then again, animals act as well, and even vegetation and minerals can move. But only man can share ideas, and godly ones at that.

So what exactly is a godly idea? Obviously we're not meant to walk around all day just reciting verses from Tanach,[4] at least not since leaving the Garden of Eden! Even something as holy as Kiddush and Havdalah uses words not found in Tanach.

It has to do with the purpose of Creation. Anything thought or said that furthers the purpose of Creation is godly. It is an expression of the will of God, and nothing is holier than that, which we clearly see from this:

> So I came today to the fountain and I said, 'O

---

4 A Hebrew acronym for Torah, Nevi'im, Kesuvim—Torah, Prophets, and Writings.

God, God of my master, Avraham, if You desire to prosper my way on which I am going… (Bereishis 24:42)

So I came today: …Rebi Acha said: The ordinary conversation of the servants of the Forefathers is more beloved before the Omnipresent than the Torah of their sons… (Rashi)

Really? And why might that be? Because everything the Avos did was done only because it was what Creation wanted in order to fulfill the purpose of its Creator? Because a servant like Eliezer knew the score and acted the same way as his master, so whatever he said somehow conveyed that purpose?

What purpose?

The Plan

three

THE MIDRASH SAYS that when God decided to make Creation, He used the Torah as the blueprint.[1] That means the entire universe, what we can see and what we can't, has been constructed according to Torah. As it says:

> Ben Bag Bag said: "Turn it over, and [again] turn it over, for all is therein. And look into it; And become gray and old therein; and do not move away from it, for you have no better portion than it." (Pirkei Avos 5:22)

Everything is in the Torah, even the most despi-

---

[1] Bereishis Rabbah 1:1.

cable parts known to history?

Yes, even that.

This means that although the Jewish people make up a very, very small portion of the world's population, and an even smaller portion of the Jewish population actually lives by Torah, Creation was made for the purpose set out therein. The world as a whole may disregard the Torah world because of its small population—and even smaller contribution to the scientific and technological advancement of mankind—but that's only for now. If it knew the true plan for Creation, its people would shift their allegiance in a flash.

However, that's not going to happen while the yetzer hara is free to roam. It's everywhere. It drives the economy. It drives relationships. It drives us crazy if we don't do what it wants, and it clearly has a say in the Torah approach to life of many today. To quote the Arizal, the yetzer hara is literally the ba'al habayis.[2]

This undermines many important qualities of being human, but one that is most affected is self-honesty. A person needs self-honesty to avoid self-dishonesty. There are a lot of people out there claiming to be doing good for the world. The question is whose world.

Self-honesty keeps arrogance in check. That's really important for a number of reasons, one of which is

---

[2] Owner of the house; Sha'ar HaGilgulim, Introduction 23.

to stop people from thinking they're smarter than everyone else—even if they are. Being smart and humble is an asset. Being smart and arrogant is a serious threat to the well-being of mankind, because those people tend to play God.

What does the Torah say about the plan for Creation?

> The verse says, "All the works of God are for His sake" (Mishlei 16:4), because everything that has been created is for His own glory. This does not mean, however, for His own end or good, God forbid. More deeply, [it means] in order to reveal His light and glory to those who are worthy of it. It is the revelation of the light and glory of God, may He be blessed, that is the pleasure, enjoyment, and radiance for all those who merit to cling to and unify with Him. This is the main enjoyment, brilliance, and pleasure of eternal life in the World-to-Come… (Chelek HaBiurim, Drushei Igulim v'Yoshar, Anaf 1, Os 1)

Wow. That is deep. It's even harder to sell. Malls are packed with people. Places of worship are not. Theaters are filled to capacity. Places of God are not. People will sacrifice much for the almighty dollar, but not for the Almighty Himself. And that's not going to change until people better understand what it means to cling to God and to unify with Him, because so far that just sounds like a lot of unimpressive religious jargon. How can that be done? By clearing up some misconceptions.

The first misconception to deal with has to do with why God made Creation and especially man. He either made Creation to help us or to hurt us. If He made Creation to hurt us, we'd all be begging to end it. Bad things do happen, but for the most part people LOVE life. That's due to God. As the Talmud says, "Everything God does is for the good."[3]

The second misconception will take a little longer to clear up. Somehow going to shul is supposed to be better than hanging out at the mall or more exhilarating than jumping from a plane. Somehow learning Torah is supposed to be more enjoyable than going to a ballgame.

Until recent times, the rebuttals would have been more theoretical than anything else. Far more Jews used to leave the fold than join it, speaking badly about Torah Judaism on their way out. An outsider could say, "You see? Once religious people taste the good life, they realize what they are missing and run to it!"

But today there are also ba'alei teshuvah, many of them—secular Jews who consciously and willingly

---

[3] Brochos 60b.

went in the other direction and became religious. And whereas once that seemed to be true only for people who could not find their places in secular society, today the ranks of ba'alei teshuvah include people who are successful even by secular standards.

The tables have turned. Now a religious person can say, "You see? Once secular people taste the good life of Torah, they realize what they were missing and run to acquire it!"

But what kind of Jew leaves Torah Judaism for a secular lifestyle, and what kind does the reverse?

There are exceptions to almost every rule, but not this one. No one to date has left Torah because he felt it was the moral thing to do, even if he said that was the reason. No society has more to say about morality than Torah Judaism, unless to people who redefine the whole concept of morality or ignore it altogether, as many have.

If anything, they might dispute its divine authenticity, regardless of whether or not they know enough about it to even question it. But that's usually because they found it easier to live without Torah. You won't get a fight from the yetzer hara over this one, nor from the seven billion other yetzer haras the world over, and ignorance finds comfort in numbers.

The main reason for such heresy is that God seemingly lets people get away with it, at least for now. He no longer overtly punishes people for straying from

Torah, and some people mistake His patience as His absence. It's an illusion—or rather a delusion—but one that someone is willing to live with when his yetzer hara is his chief life strategist.

On the other hand, what kind of Jew turns his back on an easier life for a more complicated and difficult one, one that he had to go out of his way to find? As we tell a potential convert, "Why would you give up a mitzvah-lite life for a far more intense one?"

A gentile has that choice, so we can ask him the question. A secular Jew does not have the choice, being obligated in the 613 mitzvos from the age of bar or bas mitzvah. But until he learned otherwise, he apparently thought he did. What compelled him to make the dramatic and heroic change?

Da'as. It's a game changer, a yetzer-hara killer. The right da'as in the right amount can suck the wind right out of the sails of the evil inclination, and pull a person out of himself for a far nobler cause. A little bit of knowledge may be a dangerous thing, but just a little bit of the right kind of da'as is certainly dangerous—for a yetzer hara.

Why is it that some people repent when, after once thinking they had forever to live, they suddenly find themselves with only a few minutes left? Why do so many people confronted with imminent death wax philosophical and tend to become more human rather than less human?

As mentioned, there are always exceptions to the rule, but most people who sense the end coming tend to automatically zoom in on priorities that seem far closer to the soul than to the body. It's as if they always knew about them, which they did, and having silenced the yetzer hara, which acceptance of death does, they are free to think and talk about them.

That would make da'as a goal of life. The objective is to cling to God. The means to do that is through da'as, which certainly explains why the very first test the first man and woman were given had to do with da'as, as in the forbidden fruit of the Aitz HA'DA'AS Tov v'Ra —the Tree of KNOWLEDGE of Good and Evil.

After all, had it been only man's obedience that God wanted to test, any fruit tree would have worked. Why did it have to be a tree of knowledge, and not just any knowledge, but knowledge of GOOD and knowledge of BAD? This seems to have made the test not only one of loyalty, but of specifically choosing good knowledge over bad knowledge.

Which means what?

Given the purpose of Creation, good knowledge is any knowledge that reveals God to people and inspires them to seek out a close relationship with Him. Bad knowledge is any knowledge that has the reverse effect. What was the result of Adam's eating?

They heard the voice of God going in the garden

to the direction of the sun, and the man and his wife hid from before God… (Bereishis 3:8)

Clearly they had chosen incorrectly. Despite new the knowledge that was gained from the eating, it pushed them away from God.

One of the biggest surprises for ba'alei teshuvah is that not only does another type of knowledge exist besides what they were taught in the secular world—and not only does it make great sense and answer questions about life that secular knowledge does not, at least with any certainty—but it is also super inspiring and super insightful…it's just plain SUPER.

SUPERnatural, actually. At first Torah learning just seems basic, because that is what it is. You start with a simple verse from the Torah and understand it on its most basic level. It might even seem childish, because that is usually the level at which children begin to learn…at the age of five.

Then comes Rashi.[4] He says that he only comes to help with the simple explanation of a verse or section of Talmud, and he tends to do it in very few words. But just by asking the simple question, "What's bother-

____

4 Rabbi Shlomo Yitzchaki (1040-1105), today generally known by the acronym Rashi, was a medieval French rabbi and author of a comprehensive and authoritative commentary on the Talmud and Tanach.

ing Rashi?" along with the fact that he felt compelled to say what he did and in the precise way he said it yield significant depth to the basic understanding.

The Ramban,[5] Sforno,[6] and Ibn Ezra[7] are just a few more of the pashtanim—commentators who focus on the basic understanding of a section of Torah. Their discussions not only elucidate, but also demand elucidation, and serve to greatly widen the aperture of Torah for those who learn them. One thing is certain about all these men: they were HIGHLY intelligent people, and probably head and shoulders above their counterparts.

This was certainly the case with the Ohr Ha-Chaim HaKadosh.[8] His commentary also explains the Torah on its most basic level, but it does not stop from

---

[5] Rabbi Moshe ben Nachman (1194-1270), a medieval Jewish scholar, Sephardic rabbi, philosopher, physician, kabbalist, and biblical commentator.

[6] Rabbi Ovadiah ben Ya'akov Sforno, an Italian rabbi, biblical commentator, philosopher, and physician, was born at Cesena about 1475 and died at Bologna in 1550.

[7] Rabbi Avraham ben Meir Ibn Ezra (1089-1167) was one of the most distinguished Jewish biblical commentators and philosophers of the Middle Ages. He was born in Tudela in northern Spain.

[8] Rabbi Chaim ben Moshe ibn Attar (1696-1743), known as the Or HaChaim after his popular commentary on the Torah, was a talmudist and kabbalist.

venturing far beyond, into the rest of Pardes.[9] It's a good first exposure to how, when it comes to Torah, something so simple can also be so incredibly profound.

But then again, what do you expect from the blueprint for Creation and the spice for the yetzer hara?[10] And all this is before people have learned Mishnah, moved on to Talmud, and, if they are really fortunate, entered the realm of Kabbalah!

It is also before they learned the Yad Chazakah[11] of the Rambam[12] and its myriad commentaries, as well as the countless commentaries and codifications that

---

[9] Pardes is the transliteration of the Hebrew word spelled Peh-Raish-Dalet-Samech. A pardes is actually an orchard, but in this case each letter is the first letter of its own word: Peh for Pshat–Simple, Raish for Remez–Hint, Dalet for Drush–Exegesis, and Samech for Sod–Secret. These are the four levels of Torah, from the simplest to the most kabbalistic (Sha'ar HaGilgulim, Introduction 11).

[10] See Chapter 1.

[11] The Mishneh Torah, subtitled Sefer Yad HaChazakah, is Rambam's code of Jewish religious law, based on the Talmud and compiled between 1170 and 1180 CE. It consists of 14 books, subdivided into sections, chapters, and paragraphs, which detail all Jewish observance, including laws applicable only when the Temple existed.

[12] Rabbi Moshe ben Maimon (1138-1204) was a medieval Sephardic Jewish philosopher who became one of the most prolific and influential Torah scholars of the Middle Ages. He was also a preeminent astrologer and physician.

have since followed, just to give a better handle on Torah.[13] And until this very day the commentaries have been coming up with new understandings of old ideas, being helped by the advancements of science and technology.

A person born into a Torah lifestyle is usually somewhat aware of the endless intellectual world of Torah, at least in theory. For the ba'al teshuvah, who goes even just part of the distance, it's like stumbling onto a vast and endless hidden treasure of ideas and understanding that is clearly just the portal to a higher dimension of reality, one in which GOOD da'as rules the world.

---

[13] Make it easier to grasp.

Da'as and the Moment

four

INFORMATION IS EVERYWHERE. It takes many different forms. It comes in the written word, the spoken word, or just a picture equal to a thousand words. We are filled with information and exist as a function of it. Researchers calculate that in a single moment humankind is able to store at least 295 exabytes of information, a number with 20 zeroes in it!

Just trying to grasp the magnitude of that number is enough to take your breath away and cause your circuits to short. And yet…and YET a single piece of missing information in an individual can mean the difference between crisis and no crisis, even between life and death.

Just staying healthy is a miracle. As a doctor once told a complaining patient, "Don't ask why you are sick. Ask instead why you are not sick more often!" With all the things that could go wrong in a body, it is amazing that they don't, especially given how little we know about protecting ourself.

Albert Einstein has been quoted as saying, "Two things are infinite: the universe and human stupidity, and I'm not sure about the universe." Although it turns out that both are finite, it is the latter that has resulted in misleading many people, with consequences leading to much death and destruction even among the highly intelligent.

Not that human stupidity is always obvious. On the contrary, stupidity can seem normal if enough people share the same ignorance. Not only that, but when a different way of thinking appears, it is assumed to be faulty and thus rejected, especially if it is held only by a minority.

Consider western society, which is made up of billions of people basically doing the same thing, working toward the same goals. Where did that society come from, how did it get here, and where is it going?

The answers to these questions are really the history of mankind. The same answers are also true for the eastern world, although it is a lot less uniform than the western one. Today what we see throughout mankind is for the most part basically the same thing, even though each sector has its own accent color.

The exceptions are those who claim to have received outside input, like the Jewish people with their Torah. The rest of society has been a function of live and learn, trial and error, and best guess. When something was tried and failed, it was scrapped and something else was tried instead. People continued doing that until something finally worked, at which time it was incorporated into their weltanschauung,[1] and they moved on to another problem.

The question is what it means to say that something has worked. Doesn't that depend on a society's expectations? Society may not let you run a red light because it endangers others, but it will let you do all kinds of immoral things behind closed doors, so long as they don't break any existing laws.

Many governments today are corrupt. Police forces paid to protect us don't always do an adequate job. Well-established rules are either ignored or circumvented to the detriment of the common interest. People are constantly manipulated and taken advantage of, sometimes even knowingly.

But if enough people can get up in the morning, go about more or less as they planned, and contribute to their goals in some meaningful way, society is working well enough as far as they are concerned. Glitches happen. Failures occur. But in seemingly limited

---

[1] A particular philosophy or view of life; the worldview of an individual or group.

amounts they are acceptable, and people will continue to go with the flow.

Besides, the food is good. The clothing is nice. The entertainment is enjoyable. If you're not happy, there are ways to become happy. And most important of all, there is no one credible enough to stand on a high rock and tell people how much they are underachieving and missing the point of life. Someone who tries to do that will be shouted down by people committed to leaving things the way they are—to THEIR advantage.

Everything could change in a flash if only the flash would come. In olden times it did. Things happened and there was no doubt that it was God expressing His disapproval. People knew that they had to shape up or ship out. They had their run of things for a while before the party ended and they knew it was useless, even stupid, to resist.

Not anymore. Prophecy ended 2300 years ago. We stopped listening to the prophets so God stopped talking to them. The Talmud does say that since then prophecy has been given to talmidei cha-chamim, crazy people, and perhaps even children.[2] The only problem is which talmidim chachamim. Who trusts a crazy person? Don't children tell stories? So instead, the worst punishment God gives people who choose

____

[2] Bava Basra 12a.

to ignore truth is to let them keep ignoring it. The punishment for living a fun but meaningless life is to be able to continue to live one. However, the truth will catch up later when such people can't catch up to it, and they will regret EVERYTHING.

In the meantime they will be misled…and they will mislead others. And every once in a while God may reboot history at man's expense, and frequently at the expense of the Jewish people. That usually works to correct the human arc somewhat, until the gravity of the yetzer hara once again drags mankind back to its lowly grasp of life, while moments of great spiritual opportunity pass completely unnoticed.

I once had the opportunity to drive a well-known out-of-town rabbi to a weekend retreat for a talk he was scheduled to give on a Sunday morning at 9 a.m. The organization I worked for was hosting the program, and I was asked to pick up the rabbi at a relative's home, drive him an hour or so to the retreat, wait for him, and then take him to the airport so he could return to his home in another city.

The plan was to get the rabbi early enough for him to pray with the minyan at the retreat and then have breakfast before his talk. It was carefully thought out, and I was looking forward to the opportunity to be by myself in the presence of such Torah greatness.

I arrived on time and the rabbi was ready. It was winter and still dark at 6:30 a.m. We left within moments of my arrival and after a short while I worked up enough nerve to begin asking my prepared questions, probing for insightful answers. We had been taught to always have questions ready, just in case an opportunity to ask them came up, and I was ready.

The rabbi politely answered each question as we drove north to the retreat. Everything was going according to plan, and I was getting more than my money's worth from this rare opportunity.

It was still dark and though I paid attention to the road as we spoke, I apparently missed the turnoff for the lodge. Unfortunately I did not realize it immediately, and the next turnoff was miles ahead. When it became apparent that I was lost and that we would not get to the lodge in time for minyan, the rabbi quietly prayed on his own, never once displaying a trace of disappointment or anger. Perhaps he saw that I was in a panic and left bad enough alone.

After finally turning around miles out of the way, I still did not recognize where I was going—this was before aids like Waze, Google Maps, and even cell phones—and afraid to go too far in the wrong direction, I got off the highway, not knowing whether I should or not.

As the rabbi finished praying, I kept looking for something, anything, to point me in the right direction, all the while imagining disappointed and angry people waiting for us at our destination. Hopeless and extremely dismayed, I was both shocked and relieved to suddenly see the actual lodge ahead of us!

To this day I cannot explain how we got there, because I didn't recognize anything to give even a clue as to where to turn. It was a straight-out miracle, because we also arrived literally five minutes before the rabbi was scheduled to speak. So at 9 a.m., without breakfast, the rabbi did his thing while I sat and sulked.

The rabbi didn't miss a beat, and there was no indication from the way he spoke or acted that anything had gone wrong. I drove him to the airport in silence, especially after he said, "You know, when you're driving somewhere, it is really best just to focus on the road."

In other words, that advice about having questions ready for a wise man and asking them in his presence is true only if you're not driving to a place with which you are not very familiar. At 60 miles an hour and in the dark, it is much too easy to miss an important turnoff in the blink of an eye, or even just the blink of your mind's eye.

That incident happened about 30 years ago, and I still cringe whenever I think about it, although I am still awed by the miracle of getting to the place on time. I am the kind of person who tries to turn events like this into lessons for life, and though there have been a few, this one spoke to me the most.

Life is filled with many great opportunities, as well

as many distractions from them. Sometimes you can correct mistakes later on or a miracle can happen to compensate somewhat for what went wrong, but it is still never the same as getting it right the first time.

As Shlomo HaMelech wisely wrote, everything has its time[3] and every person has his hour.[4] Everything is a function of Divine Providence, and once something happens, it is b'shert, not to mention that all God does He does for the good,[5] though there is something called alillus.[6]

Nevertheless, there is such a thing as taking advantage of an opportunity or missing one. There is such a thing as doing a mitzvah or committing a sin and being held accountable for it. The whole difference between the good and the bad often comes down to what you were aware of at the moment of truth, of not being the crazy person or the unwise person who did not care to see what was being born.[7]

I remember watching TV and seeing Apollo 11 take off and later land on the moon. It was dramatic, and amazingly everything went quite smoothly as far

---

[3] Koheles, Ch. 3.

[4] Pirkei Avos 4:3.

[5] Brochos 61b.

[6] A situation in which we make mistakes that seem to have been set up by God for some reason we may not yet understand (Drushei Olam HaTohu, Chelek 2, Drush 4, Anaf 18, Siman 3).

[7] See the Introduction.

as the average person was concerned. As a 10-year-old, for me it was just a matter of building a rocket ship, launching three men into space, setting them on a course for the moon, getting them to land and walk around on it, launch them off the moon, meet up with the mother ship, and then head home. Simple as pie.

Many years later I read about the mission. I had already come to realize how naive I had been at the time, but the article gave me an even better appreciation of the millions of things that had to be anticipated, built, and calculated correctly. So very many things could have gone wrong, many of them based on physics equations. It was a technological miracle that everything came off so well.

Not that the people at Mission Control in Houston or those at the homes of the astronauts didn't have knots in their stomachs at different times throughout the mission. Not that there weren't moments when authorities and scientists didn't wonder to themselves, "Did we get all the math right?"

Maybe they didn't. But they got enough of it right for the astronauts to touch down on the moon and safely get back home again. Obviously there were backup plans, but even those could have failed out in space where, despite all the knowns, there are still more unknowns. Even the health of the astronauts could unexpectedly change mid-flight.

One thing is for certain though. The mission succeeded, technically speaking, because of what people knew and made a point of knowing to greatly increase the chances of success at the rare opportunity. The amount of research, discussions and late-night meetings that went into the Apollo 11 mission must have been staggering, but it was all necessary for the sake of new knowledge built on old knowledge.

How many people involved apply the same kind of thinking to their own personal lives? How many give thought to all the opportunities that might have passed them by because they approach life like a boat on a river that cannot be controlled, but only navigated? How many people do research, have discussions, and stay up late to make sure that they are ready for any life opportunities that may come their way?

It is amazing how someone can tell you about the mechanics of a rocket engine but little about the meaning of life. It is curious how a person can be a savvy businessman and yet unsophisticated when it comes to succeeding at life itself. It is impressive how hard someone will work for a medal, and yet give up early on the purpose of life.

The reason is obvious. Bad information about a rocket engine kills people and cancels missions. An unprepared businessman will never really succeed. A medal leads to all kinds of fame and fortune. There is plenty of incentive to succeed at things for which failure is obviously costly.

But what about failure at life? What is it anyway? It depends on whom you ask. If you ask the yetzer tov, it means not living up to being b'tzelem Elokim, in the image of God.[8] But if you ask the yetzer hara, failure is not managing to have a good time in the material world, which you can certainly do by being spiritually mediocre.

Remember the show called Let's Make A Deal? Contestants were randomly chosen from the audience and given an opportunity to win various potential prizes. The best they could do was guess and take a chance, since the prizes were hidden until after their choices were made.

Sometimes people scored big, going from nothing to something great in a matter of moments. Sometimes the opposite happened. They started without anything and ended up with next to it, like hundreds of dollars worth of dog food for a pet they neither had nor wanted.

The worst and most distressing part of the show was when a contestant not only chose the wrong door but was then shown what was behind the door he didn't choose, a bonanza like an all-expense paid trip to a luxury resort as well as cash to spend! Even though he had started with nothing, the fact that with a single choice he could have ended up with such a big

---

8 Bereishis 1:26.

something, was sooooo painful, both for the one who lost out and for everyone who saw it happen.

Life is very much the same except that we don't usually get to see what's behind the other door until we are about to leave this world. Then it's revealed to us what life is truly about and what we could have done to reach a lofty goal. No one but no one at that time EVER says, "So what! I have no regrets after living a less meaningful life."

On the contrary, the final thoughts are more likely to be something like "OH MY, what was I thinking? Why didn't I care more about my direction in life? Why didn't someone tell me what life was really about? I could have had that, and instead I had this!"

The difference was just a matter of a little da'as at the time of the moment.

Celebration
of Da'as
five

THIS BRINGS US to the holiday of Shavuos, otherwise known as zman Toraseinu—the time of our Torah. It is the second of the shalosh regalim,[1] occurring 50 days after Pesach and about half a year before Succos. As the second word indicates, it is the time we celebrate our receiving of Torah at Mt. Sinai on the sixth day of Sivan, 2448, or 1313 BCE.

The only problem is that we didn't actually receive all "our Torah" on the sixth of Sivan of that year. By the fifth of Sivan we had already received some of the laws at Marah—from the beginning of the Exodus

---

[1] Literally "three legs," because Pesach, Shavuos, and Succos are like three legs of a tripod, and we went up to the Temple, usually by foot, on each of the holidays to bring the holiday offerings.

until the giving of the Torah—as set out in Sefer Bereishis and Sefer Shemos. On the sixth of Sivan we received the Ten Commandments. We weren't supposed to receive the rest of Torah, with the vast majority of the 613 mitzvos, until 40 days later on the 16th of Tammuz. That was when Moshe Rabbeinu was scheduled to return with the first set of tablets that had been "carved out by God and engraved by God."

We lost that opportunity because the Erev Rav built the golden calf. Consequently, when Moshe came down the mountain with the first set of tablets and saw the sinning going on in the camp,[2] he ended up smashing them before we could receive them. It would take another 80 days for him to convince God to forgive the people and present the nation with a second set of tablets and the rest of the Torah.

So what are we really celebrating on Shavuos, when many stay up all night solely to learn Torah and receive it again on a personal level?

Another question. God told Moshe before he descended the mountain what to expect in the camp below. In fact He dismissed Moshe for that very reason, blaming him for taking out the Erev Rav, who caused all the trouble.[3] So why did Moshe take the tablets with him, and not just leave them on the mountain until

---

[2] Shemos 32:1.
[3] Rashi, Shemos 32:7.

everything in the camp below was made right?

No one would ever consider throwing down a Sefer Torah to make any point at all to any congregation. On the contrary, if someone lifting the Sefer Torah looks even a bit unsteady, people will dive to support the Torah and protect it from falling. And a Sefer Torah is only animal parchment, prepared by man and written on by man. The tablets were carved out and written by God!

There's still another question. According to the midrash, the letters flew up off the tablets when Moshe Rabbeinu saw what was going on down below. Until that time the tablets had basically carried themselves, because no human being could have carried that heavy a weight in his arms. The words engraved on the stones gave them a miraculous quality.[4]

Yet the Torah says that Moshe threw down the tablets.[5] It sounds more as if they threw themselves down when the Jewish people lost the merit to receive them. How can the midrash be reconciled with the actual verse from the Torah? And why did God thank Moshe as if he did in fact throw down and break the tablets?[6]

There is one answer to all these questions: da'as.

---

4 Tanchuma, Ki Sisa 26.

5 Shemos 32:19.

6 Shabbos 87a.

It all has to do with da'as. Not just any da'as, but the kind alluded to in the fourth blessing of the Shemoneh Esrai:

> You graciously bestow da'as on man and teach mortals understanding…Blessed are You, God, gracious bestower of da'as.

Average people would probably interpret this to mean that learning anything is a gift from God, and they are right. Many people are born impaired in one way or another, which prevents them from being able to learn—a central part of a fulfilling life. And since we have little or no control over our inborn abilities and health, having any of them is a great gift.

That's why average people can say this blessing quickly and without much consideration. It's not that they disagree with it but rather that they don't feel dependent on God to learn since they seem to be able to get knowledge easily on their own. And today that feeling is intensified with online education.

People who are above average know otherwise. They agree that ALL learning is a gift, not just part of everyday life as it is for the average person. But they also know that having da'as is only the first level of miracle, as well as the less obvious one. They know that there is something beyond small-d da'as. There is capital-d da'as—Da'as.

This is the Da'as that Shlomo HaMelech tells us about when he writes:

> If you want it like money and pursue it like treasures, then…Da'as Elokim you will find. (Mishlei 2:4-5)

Hmm. I love knowledge. I love to learn. But I can't say that the last time I felt compelled to attend a class it was with a force equal to my drive for money or for buried treasure I might happen to hear about. I wish. On the contrary, it is not unlike me to find a book I need and casually look at it with a cup of coffee and a piece of cake.

But Da'as Elokim is a different story. I know that it is not something easily achieved. I know that it is a portal to higher realms of understanding. I recognize that it is a level of wisdom that goes far beyond any other knowledge known to man, and that you can't just get it whenever you want to. Only God decides who gets access to this level of da'as, no matter how hard someone may try on his own.

This is alluded to here:

God saw that the light was good, and God separated between the light and the darkness. (Bereishis 1:4)

God separated: He saw that the wicked were

unworthy of using [the light] and therefore set it apart for the righteous in the future time (Chagigah 12a). (Rashi)

He made a separation in the illumination of the light, that it should not flow or give off light except for the righteous, whose actions draw it down and make it emanate. However, the actions of the evil block it, leaving them in darkness, and this itself was the hiding of the light. (Sefer HaKlallim, Klal 18, Anaf 8:4)

Hence the light's kabbalistic name and nature, Ohr HaGanuz—hidden light. It originates so high up in the system, on a level called Da'as Elyon—Upper Da'as—that we can never access it while still in our physical body. This is what God basically told Moshe Rabbeinu:

You will not be able to see My face, for man shall not see Me and live. (Shemos 33:20)

A person's face is one of the highest levels of the body. What is more important, it reveals on the outside what is hidden on the inside, as the Hebrew word panim hints. The highest level of divine revelation awaits us in much later periods of history, well into Olam HaBa—the World-to-Come.

In the meantime we can access only aspects of

that light, each person according to his spiritual worthiness. Just as glasses can improve and sharpen a person's vision of reality and therefore his interpretation of it, the Ohr HaGanuz does the same thing for the mind's eye.

It's difficult for people to comprehend that what they see is not necessarily the truth about what exists, even though they seem to experience proof of this every day. How many witnesses have testified to seeing something that in the end turned out to be an impossibility? How many times have people sworn to have seen something that was found to never have been there? This happens often and to just about anyone.

Mistaken perceptions are not usually a result of poor or limited eyesight. Everything that physically could have been seen was seen. The mistaken perceptions are a function of missing information, or a misunderstanding of known information, the result of which is a mental distortion of hard cold facts.

The danger of this is obvious. It is one thing to be wrong about life. It is far more dangerous to be wrong about life and think you are right about it. It is one thing to lie. It is more insidious to lie and think it is the actual truth. Without Da'as, this happens frequently and rather automatically, thanks to the yetzer hara.

All that changed for the Jewish people at Mt. Sinai. But it happened in one moment, a moment that is famous, but not for this per se. The Jewish people gained the right to Da'as Elokim at that moment:

> He [Moshe] took the Book of the Covenant and read it within the hearing of the people, and they said, "All that God said, we will do and we will hear." (Shemos 24:7)

It doesn't seem like much, and perhaps that is what anyone would have said under the circumstances. But the Talmud says otherwise:

> Rebi Simai taught: When the Jewish said "we will do" before "we will hear," 600,000 ministering angels came and tied two crowns to each member of the Jewish people, one corresponding to "we will do" and one corresponding to "we will hear." (Shabbos 88a)

That was quite a reaction from heaven. In fact the Talmud says that God even refers to their answer as the secret of angels. As the Talmud points out elsewhere,[7] most people would never agree to accept anything as comprehensive as Torah without first knowing all the details. Somehow, when the Jewish people answered as they did, it was with a level of

---

[7] Kesuvos 112a.

da'as that surpassed that of mortal men, and they even became immortal as a result. The Har Sinai experience had allowed them to tap into Da'as Elyon, at least temporarily.

As the Talmud concludes, the sin of the golden calf cost them what they had gained. They lost their heavenly crowns, became mortal once again, and the rest has been a long and often arduous history.

Well, not exactly.

"You only get one shot at a first impression," and Moshe Rabbeinu was determined to use this one to the best of his ability. He knew that the Jewish people lost the chance to receive Torah on the level he was bringing down, and probably wouldn't have another opportunity again for a long time. So he made a point of at least showing them what they almost received before they lost it.

We can't comprehend what that must have looked like to the Jewish people, because there is nothing in our experience that can compare to it. But the Pri Tzaddik says that even this very short exposure to the first set of tablets engraved Torah on the hearts of the Jewish people and continues to carry us to this very day.[8] It's what saved the traces of our incredible transformation from disappearing altogether.

That alone is cause for great celebration. But

---

8 Pri Tzaddik, Ki Sisa.

there is more. Seeing the first set of tablets didn't just give us an indelible connection to Torah—it allowed us to maintain access to Da'as. That is why God approved of Moshe Rabbeinu's independent act of bringing the tablets down and letting them be destroyed. It was, in the language of Shabbos law, "destruction for the sake of building," and that makes Shavuos a joyous event despite what did not occur.

WE MAY NEVER know how many catastrophes and tragedies have occurred because someone made the wrong split-second decision. He might have been caught totally off-guard, or even just partially, but the element of surprise was enough to make his brain stall and leave him vulnerable to error.

Not every bad decision has an immediate impact, and not every impact is fully understood at the time. Sometimes a wrong turn in life can take years before it is clear that it was the wrong one, and longer until it is clear at what cost. By that time the person may have changed too much to appreciate the mistake or care to do anything about it.

It is frightening and amazing how a single momentary decision can lead to so much bad for so many people. Could World War II and the Holocaust have been avoided had British Prime Minister Chamberlain not tried to appease Adolf Hitler, ysv"z? Could Pearl Harbor have been prevented had the Americans taken the Japanese threat more seriously?

There are stories of Jews who had months to flee Europe before the Holocaust began but chose to stay put and died as a result. Others had only moments to decide to leave, and they immediately dropped everything, fled with only what they could carry, and survived. Between 1933 and 1939 the Nazis allowed Jews to leave for Palestine;[1] 60,000 left Germany and survived. The remaining 100,000 German Jews rejected the offer and met one terrible fate or another.

There is no denying that everything is a matter of Hashgochah Pratis, Divine Providence. This is especially clear when things go our way when they really shouldn't, or don't when we think they really should. God has His master plan, and no one but no one can every do anything to interfere with it. It will always prevail.

But—and this is an extremely important but—it doesn't necessarily mean that a particular person has to be a shaliach[2] for either good or bad. Just like any

---

[1] By the Haavara Agreement between Nazi Germany and Zionist German Jews.

[2] Emissary or agent.

story, God's plan can be carried out by any number of qualified players, each having his own merit to receive a part. As it says, "God merits the meritorious,"[3] and likewise uses those lacking merit to do His less favorable work.

Merit? What merit?

Everyone's life is different because everyone IS different. We all also grow up under different circumstances, which means that no two people ever really respond exactly the same way to the same situation. But we're all equal in one very important respect, and that is in our ability to choose how to handle each situation.

For example if I have $50, I can choose to buy something for $50 or less. If I spend it all, I've spent the most I can spend. If I only have $40, I can never match the person with $50 in amount, but if I spend all of it, then I too will have spent the most I can spend. We'll be equal in that respect.

The same thing is true when it comes to free will. Everyone has free will, but the amount of free will each one has depends on many factors, most of which are known only to God. The only thing we will be judged for is how much of our personal capacity for free will we use when making each and every decision, and especially the important ones.

---

[3] Sifrei Beha'alosecha 1:22.

This is the merit we either earn or squander. A good decision is not just one that brings us material or emotional benefit, and a bad one is not just one that does the reverse. Many times the exact opposite is true.

For some, just knowing that a decision positively helped someone or something in some way is compensation enough. Losing something may still smart, but not very much, because doing good makes these people feel good.

For others it is not so easy. Knowing that they did the right thing doesn't always overcome their sense of loss or anticipated sense of loss. Telling them they will earn much more reward because of their decision—in a world they can neither see nor confirm—doesn't speak loudly enough to their emotions. They will either do the selfish thing or regret that they didn't, especially when what they missed becomes apparent or they find they really need the money they gave up.

It hurts to say and even more to hear, but greed runs the world. Selfish interests fuel the economy's momentum. The amount varies from person to person, but average people work for themselves and have to be cajoled to think of others first—which is okay according to the standards of the secular world. Although selfless generosity is not the norm, it's considered to be a stellar trait, usually found mostly among those who can afford to be that way.

The same is true in the Torah world, although perhaps to a lesser degree. Such people are raised with the concept of giving charity, tithes, etc. They are taught from a young age about mitzvos to care about their fellow man and to lend a helping hand when people are in dire need. They might even be familiar on some level with the idea that everything they have is in fact a gift from God—tzedakah—and therefore not really their own.[4]

Everything we have, the Talmud says, is only in our possession for the sake of doing the will of God, because that is what earns us eternal reward in the World-to-Come, which is the whole purpose of Creation. We are only bnei Olam HaZeh, people of this world, waiting to become bnei Olam HaBa, people of the next world.

> This world is like a corridor before the World-to-Come... (Pirkei Avos 4:16)

But how many Torah Jews think like this on a day-to-day basis? If they're living spiritual lives cut off from the material world around them, perhaps all the time. But if they're part of the fast-paced material-oriented world, how can they not get swept up by it? Many are forced to come up with unnatural and even perverted

---

4 Brochos 17a.

syntheses of two usually very opposite worlds.[5]

Even if people do somehow balance out the physical and material worlds, there is no guarantee that their spouses or children will. Some rationalizations may not even be for the people themselves, but rather for their relatives whom they have a more difficult time keeping in spiritual line.

It all comes down to their level of Da'as, of how deeply people know the truth and have taken it to heart. There are people who eat unhealthy food but have no idea how bad it is for them. There are others who continue to eat food that is unhealthy even after they learn of its dangers.

And then there are the few people for whom the knowledge of potential danger is enough to effect a change to their diets, and they begin to eat more healthy foods. The fact that something can go wrong is close enough to its actually going wrong to intimidate them into taking fewer risks to their health.

The current pandemic is a recent case in point. Stay in the house or don't stay in the house; wear a mask in public or don't wear the mask in public. The population is divided between the cautious and the reckless, those who abide by the rules and those who do not, those who care about others and those who don't think too much about them.

---

[5] Brochos 5b.

You can be sure that there would be a lot of converts to the side of the cautious if people were to watch the stages of COVID-19 death. There should be some kind of simulator to let healthy people feel the effects of the infection, so they would know what to expect if they caught it. That could provide some extra oomph to push some warnings from the mind—where they are not felt—to the heart, where they are.

The Shemoneh Esrai mentions three levels of Da'as: dayah, binah, and haskel. The first is more like plain factual knowledge, what you get when you learn something without really relating to it. Binah is understanding, which tends to follow after an effort to make sense of the facts. It might evoke an emotional response or it might not. That depends on the idea and the person.

Haskel is the level of knowing in which the idea rings so true to people that they adjust their lives accordingly. The ideas may not necessarily be ones people would give up life to uphold, but they will certainly be willing to make sacrifices to keep them, like wearing a mask when it is uncomfortable because it is clearly the safer and more considerate way to go.

It all comes down to one very important idea: how much people believe in truth and are willing to live by it. They could ask themselves in any situation, "What is the truth here?" especially when it comes to the more difficult moral decisions in life. Those are the ones that the yetzer hara fights against the most, making rationalization more likely.

Asking that question changes everything. It really focuses people on what they're doing, and draws their consciousness more into the picture. It's amazing how much we do without being really present consciously, almost as if we're spectators to someone else's actions. Zeroing in on the truth is a great way for us to remind ourself that we are no spectator. We are the EVENT.

Once again it brings us back to Da'as. You can't know the truth without Da'as because the two are basically the same thing. Knowing this on some subconscious level doesn't qualify as knowing enough at the moment to tailor your actions according to it.

A child knows full well the prohibition against sneaking a cookie from the jar before supper. But it is only when his mother surprises him and says, "Just what do you think you're doing?" that the wrongness of his action surfaces in his conscious mind, and with it the potential consequences of the forbidden act.

As some have noted, many of us don't actually grow up. We just learn better how to act in public, which for some means learning to be better at camouflaging inappropriate actions. Or some just learn to become more sophisticated rationalizers, better able to convince themselves that they do no wrong, or that their wrong is not so bad anyhow.

Question: If a video were circulating that showed

the horrible path to death of a COVID-19 sufferer, would it make any converts to wearing masks? If there were a way to let people feel the pain, would it change their approach? If the spread of germs could be simulated in a real and convincing way, wouldn't careful people become even more careful?

How much Da'as does it take to actually change a person?

Clearly the answer depends on the person and the situation. If the situation is serious and the person is serious, it doesn't take much Da'as to inspire him to respond appropriately. If the person is serious but the situation is not, then he might need Da'as in order not to over-react, which is not the worst outcome.

But if the person isn't serious and the situation is, then he will likely under-react, and that CAN be and often IS dangerous. Someone will need a LOT of Da'as to turn himself around and respond correctly, and frankly that is asking for trouble.

God wants us to be responsible people. It is godly to be so, and it is the way we partner with Him to help Creation reach its intended goal. This means responding to the needs of history sensibly in an appropriate manner. He'll forgive us for being overly cautious, but He'll send crises our way if we aren't cautious enough.

Historically major disasters have often followed on the heels of morally reckless times. As it says:

[He is] the One Who teaches man Da'as....Fortunate is the man whom You, God, chastise, and from Your Torah You teach him. To grant him peace from days of evil, while a pit is dug for the wicked. (Tehillim 94:10, 12-13)

The Talmud states it like this:

Rebi Avin HaLevi said: If one forces the moment [and attempts to take advantage of an undeserved opportunity, the] moment will force him [and he will be pushed aside]. If one yields to the moment [and correctly relinquishes an opportunity that presents itself, the] moment will yield to him. (Brochos 64a)

It can be compared to holding a $100 bill in your hand. On the surface, it's just a piece of paper, not even worth its monetary value. But its potential to purchase all kinds of life-enhancing articles makes it a powerful and desired commodity. It can generate a lot of excitement and enjoyment just sitting in the person's hand.

Moments of life are like that too. Sitting in our hand, they can seem almost worthless. But with the right amount of Da'as Elohim, we can become acutely aware of the power of each moment that passes, creating excitement and providing enjoyment as we consider its potential to enhance the quality of our life.

Without Da'as, a moment is just a moment. Billions of moments are squandered each second for this reason. But with Da'as, a moment has the potential to become THE moment of moments, taking us to a whole new and higher level of living. Is there really any question about the way to go?

There Will Come a Time

seven

WE HAVE BEEN living through very tumultuous times. Most of us alive today did not live through World War II and the Holocaust; the majority of those who did have already died. More recently we have had a good run of history, relatively peaceful and constructive compared to what came before.

Not that we haven't had wars, terrible terrorist attacks, economic crises, and even epidemics. No period will be perfect until the Messianic Era. But as far as history has been going, for many people this current period has had more positive, favorable moments than negative, unfavorable ones. Life has been good for a greater percentage of the population than in previous millennia.

Then came COVID-19. Overnight the dangerous

coronavirus grew into a pandemic, and for the first time in a long while worldwide protective measures had to be implemented, measures that greatly curbed civil liberties. The complacent Torah world was thrown into emergency mode as it tried to comply with both Torah and governmental regulations.

Both in Israel and the United States the politics have been rough. The leaders of both countries have had to continuously fight the opposition just to govern. Personal and party mandates seem to have become more important than the people they are supposed to serve, and the media has done its part to make sure that the chaos and confusion unsettle the population.

It has been crazy in America. The Democrats did not expect to lose the election, and when the shock of that reality wore off somewhat, they went to war against the democratically elected president, Donald Trump. They relentlessly did everything they could—which apparently included breaking the law and making horrific false accusations—to undermine his presidency, at GREAT expense to the American people.

During the previous presidency, the Democrats clearly implemented a mission to liberalize the country. They reduced religious influence in everyday life while permitting activities and ways of life that were previously taboo—not only because people were trained to look at them that way but because they were innately unnatural.

Had the president at that time legally been allowed a third term, which he hinted he would like, he would have continued that mandate, supported by the liberal and manipulative media. They certainly would have voted for him, because liberalism is to their own advantage as well. It doesn't get much more liberal than in Hollywood.

That was one amendment the president's supporters could not get passed, and time ran out on his presidency. So it was left to his Secretary of State and political protégé to continue with the Democrat's legacy of liberalism.

When the unthinkable happened and Donald Trump won the election, panic ensued. The opposition all of a sudden found themselves on the defensive and EXTREMELY vulnerable. It didn't help that the outsider was going to Washington with his own mandate, to drain the swamp that Washington had become.

They used just about everything at their disposal to get rid of the president, and even things that should not have been at its disposal. They tried to implicate the Russians in election rigging and somehow tie it back to the Trump Administration.

Even if the Russians were involved in the extremely incriminating leaks, the truth that became known should have been enough to prove that the Democrats at the time were unworthy of national power, or of any power for that matter. If the Russians were behind the cyberattack on the Democratic National Headquarters, the American people should be indebted to them.

In the end the Russian investigation flopped and the Trump Administration survived, all the while running the country with considerable efficiency while being selfishly and unnecessarily hindered by the Democrats. It only makes sense if their intention all along had been to prevent President Trump from doing the job he was elected to do in order to dispose of him by almost any means.

When nothing else worked, the Democrats tried the impeachment angle. More taxpayer dollars. More biased media support. More distractions from the true needs of the people and responsibilities of the government. But Trump survived it all and continued to do his job despite the efforts of the opposition to see to it that he couldn't.

On the heels of the impeachment failure came the coronavirus. Just a coincidence? It was certainly Hashgochah Pratis, and a new opportunity to wear down the president and try to make him look inept before the country. In earlier periods of national crisis opposing parties put aside their differences to tend to their common interest, the welfare of the people they are supposed to be governing and protecting.

This time, instead of uniting with their counterparts for the good of the country, the Democrats saw in coronavirus a new and unused angle to chip away at the president and his ability to rule. It was as if the virus were custom-made just for them, so they could use a real national crisis as a way to once again try to bog down the president and keep him from what he had been trying to do the entire time, restoring the country to its former greatness.

And since the crisis was bound to slow down the economy, they felt justified in using that as a reason to continue to gnaw away at the Trump presidency when he should have been allowed to focus entirely on the crisis at hand. But alas, when economists began speaking about a rebound economy that would look healthier than many others in the past, the Democrats shuddered.

In the meantime something else happened. Scandal. It somehow came out—and was becoming clearer each day—that the Democrats had not only cooked up the idea of Russian collusion, but had locked up an innocent man for it, even using the FBI to do it. All of a sudden there were suspicions of great corruption all the way to the top, even to the previous president himself.

All that should have been enough for the American people to say to the Democrats and their liberal supporting media, "Keep quiet! Go back and clean up your own acts. You need to stop your power-mongering and get back to doing what you're being paid exorbitant amounts of money to do—look out for OUR best interests."

It didn't happen. Before it even could, something else did happen…seemingly out of nowhere. Some police officer in sleepy Minneapolis mistreated a black suspect, causing his death. Though the officer was tried and jailed, the country broke out in violent riots and terrible looting.

But then people reported that in cities where the rioting took place, piles of bricks suddenly, mysteriously, and conveniently showed up! This made some people assume the obvious, that either all or part of the rioting had been set up. The black man's death at the hands of a white officer was only the pretext for some other nefarious political goal.

Fingers are being pointed although it is unclear who or what is really behind the chaos. But once again Democrats and anti-Trump GOP members have rushed to try to use this latest crisis against the president, again hoping to undermine his ability as leader of waning superpower.

On the other side of the ocean the situation has been less dramatic but quite similar in ways. The liberals in Israel want more control to implement their liberal mandates, and the current prime minister and his supporters, especially the religious ones, are in the way. So they too have been working hard to get rid of the prime minister one way or another.

The miracle has been that, like President Trump, the prime minister has still been able to manage the country with hands tied behind his back. He remains in power despite major efforts by the liberals and their supportive media to push him out, including announcing apparent scandals that should make him legally unfit to serve. The fact that he is still in office defies credibility and can only be, seemingly, the result of Divine Providence.

That is also interesting because there have been predictions by some well respected rabbis and kabbalists that he would be the last prime minister before Moshiach comes. We came within inches of another election that was predicted not to come, and it didn't.

Those who forced the previous election thought that it was to their advantage to undermine the Likud's hold on power. But amazingly they only empowered the prime minister more, and they ended up pushing themselves farther into the political wings. They're probably just as baffled as the rest of us, and a lot more frustrated.

But chaos reigns here too, thanks to the coronavirus. Shuls and yeshivos were shut down, the heart of the Torah world, and God-fearing individuals have been taken suddenly. All are crucial for keeping the world going. A lot has been left to the individual during these times of quarantine and watchfulness.

At the same time businesses and parnassah have

taken great hits. Though some have found ways to compensate, maybe even use the situation to their advantage, others have had to find ways just to stay afloat and not lose their businesses. It hasn't been easy, and it won't become much easier for some time, especially as caution is still necessary.

We haven't even mentioned Europe, England, Canada, and countless other countries around the world, and how it has affected them. But we don't have to for this discussion because it is not an overview of current events. It is an introduction to the main event, something the Torah calls tohu and we call chaos.

We don't like chaos, even though we are often the cause of it. But it has its role to play in history, and it's an important one. If anything, it is a harbinger of impending redemption. Increased severity of slavery before the plagues in Egypt, Haman before the redemption in Bavel, Greek oppression before the miracle of Chanukah, and the Holocaust and World War II before the founding of the State of Israel.

God made the world that way too. Even though the second verse of the Torah discusses chaos after Creation, the Zohar explains that historically tohu-chaos actually preceded Creation.[1] The order of the six days of Creation was pulled out from the chaos that preceded it.

---

[1] Zohar, Bereishis 16a.

The Talmud says that God made the existence of Creation conditional on the Jewish people's acceptance of Torah,[2] which happened on the sixth of Sivan in 2448/1313 BCE. But as we see from history, chaos wasn't a one-time event, thanks to persecution, assimilation, and the yetzer hara. Like all bad guys, if you don't destroy them, they always lurk around the corner, waiting for a moment of weakness to attack again.

There is a reason we have governments and police forces. As civil as we'd like to believe we are or have become, the real truth is that we all have yetzer haras and, given the right set of circumstances, they can quite naturally come out and create havoc. People who lose the will to control themselves go to pieces and do VERY uncivil things.

So chaos is a good indicator of where the world is holding with respect to seder—order. It is also a good indication of how much divine help we are getting because, in all truth, we're not yet smart enough or spiritually well equipped enough to keep the world together without it. And if Torah dissipates too much for any reason, then you can be sure God will pull back as well, and chaos will ensue.

It also depends on when chaos occurs. For example, the chaos that may occur immediately before a redemption is supposed to come, specifically the FI-

---

[2] Shabbos 88a.

NAL redemption, may also be a historic announcement of redemption.

This has to do with a kabbalistic concept. There are two energies in Creation—chassadim and gevuros. The first, chassadim, are named from the word chesed–kindness and are compared to water. The gevuros, from the word gevurah–strength are compared to fire. These comparisons give good insight into the nature of each. Just as fire is indispensable and must be harnessed for good, the gevuros must also be harnessed for good.

For example, gevuros are the basis of strict behavior and can lead to much destruction. But they are also the basis of the self-discipline necessary for accomplishment in life. The energy of strict behavior and self-discipline is the same, except that in the former case the gevuros are running the show. In the case of self-discipline, people who have harnessed the energy of the gevuros use them to do their constructive bidding.

In a sense history is like some long ongoing game show. In game shows contestants often have to accomplish some specific and challenging task while racing against the clock. If time runs out, they lose. If they achieve the goal with time remaining, they win.

History also runs according to a clock, a divine clock. It began ticking with the creation of man and will end when the purpose of Creation has been sufficiently fulfilled. Generations come and go, but each one merely picks up where the previous one left off, until God's clock goes off and ends the game."

What is the challenge? To sweeten all the gevuros in Creation, a kabbalistic term for rectification of the gevuros. There are a certain amount of unrectified gevuros in the world at any given time, and when all of them have been depleted and can no longer be used for evil, Moshiach will end all history as we know it.[3]

How is this done? Basically in one of two ways. Every time we fight off our yetzer hara, which is rooted in the gevuros, we sweeten gevuros. Every time we do something good instead of bad, gevuros are rectified. Even just fighting off drowsiness to get out of bed in the morning on time to make a minyan sweetens gevuros, as does the performance of any mitzvah. The greater the moral struggle fought, the more gevuros stand to be rectified.

When we sin, the gevuros not only win but also get stronger, which increases their influence and power in the world. When the strength of the gevuros becomes overwhelmingly strong, world wars result, and they last until enough suffering has occurred to again tame the gevuros.

Because that is what suffering does—it sweetens gevuros among other benefits. Punishment for a sin is

---

3 Sha'ar HaGilgulim, Introduction 20.

not just payback, but also a means to sweeten the gevuros we failed to rectify when we acquiesced to the yetzer hara and sinned. The gevuros will either be rectified by us or through us.

Creation stops being a game show when its objective is reached, one way or another. History has deadlines that will always be met, even if heaven has to step in and do something spectacular to make them happen. If a certain number of gevuros must be rectified by a certain time so the next stage of history can follow, and we're not keeping the pace, then something will happen to make up the difference…usually at our cost, as many examples show.

There is another point to be made. Though the gevuros, like the chassadim, are just a type of divine light and energy, they are understood to have some form of awareness, or at least behave as if they do. Apparently they can sense on some level when their end is near. They exist for the sake of our free will[4] and resist tikun, fighting against it…like a cat trapped between its assailant and a wall.

This means that at the End-of-Days the gevuros are going to lash out every which way.[5] Sensing their

---

[4] The gevuros exist to give us a choice between good and evil. They put up a fight to give us a greater opportunity to harness their energy for good, by doing the moral thing.

[5] In reality it is the Sitra Achra behind them, the angel responsible to oppose man so that man can fight back and use his free will.

end, they're going to put up the fight of their life. If anyone will try the Philistine method of taking everyone else down with them, it is the gevuros. And though they won't be able to do it on a total scale, they usually are able to take down a lot of people on their way out, as they already have done and will continue to do.

The last time there was so much worldwide chaos was during World War II. Jews represented about one-twelfth of all who died in the Holocaust, and the destruction to Europe was devastating. The Japanese saw to it that as distant as America was from the shores of conflict, it was still close enough to be included in its destructive effects.

As far as Jews were concerned, WWII ended the European Exile, which was just the extended fourth and final Roman Exile. And of course the internationally accepted official reestablishment of the Jewish homeland followed on its heels in 1948, on a Jewish date that the Vilna Gaon had taught was one of redemption.[6]

This prompted many to say that Eretz Yisroel was built on the ashes of the Holocaust. And so often that is the case when it comes to geulah—redemption. There is destruction for the sake of building, at least

---

[6] The 5th of Iyar is always the 20th day of the Omer, which is Yesod sh'b'Tifferes, kabbalistically redemptive energy.

when the divine quota of gevuros requiring rectification before a particular stage of geulah—a keitz—has not been reached because of us. It then has to happen through us…again.

And here we are today. Some think redemption can still be hundreds of years off, if not longer. But they just haven't seen the sources that say otherwise, or paid close enough attention to what has been happening throughout history, especially recently. They see, but only through uninformed eyes, sharing a perception of reality that is fit to print in the newspapers.

They see politicians they like and ones they hate, some who are corrupt and others who still seem honorable. They see human beings with human tendencies do what human beings usually do in certain kinds of scenarios. They see chaos that has a habit of resurfacing from time to time, in one form or another, all in a very natural way.

They certainly don't think in terms of chassadim and gevuros, or know that the former have to be used to fix the latter. They don't see any real historic timeline or feel any clock ticking down per se. Redemption is a general concept, one they believe is best left in the hands of God, while we, mankind, just go about life as we have been taught to do, or reject how we were taught to go about it.

Because if those in the Diaspora thought otherwise, they would be RUSHING to get to Eretz Yisroel today. They would probably just take what they could and leave the rest, as Jews eventually had to do in Europe—at least those who escaped in time. If everyone thought like this, they would ALL be RUSHING to do teshuvah…doing mitzvos with more mesiras nefesh–self-sacrifice and dovening with a lot more seriousness.

The geulah plane is landing. The flaps have opened and the wheels have been lowered. At this stage of the flight even the attendants have to sit down and buckle up, and the pilots tense up as they confront one of the more stressful parts of their job. How much more so when the winds are fighting against your plane.

There will come a time in this whole process of reaching the long-awaited goal of Creation, redemption and sincere Torah-life worldwide, when we will have a choice to make. It can take days, maybe even years to get there, but a moment will come when we'll have to make a decision one way or another, and it will determine our fate from that point onward.

A single moment.

A single choice.

The truth is that many have already made it, most without even being aware of it. It took some in the direction of redemption and they are exactly where they need to be at this tumultuous stage of history. Others made a choice that pushed them far away from redemption, as is beginning to become clearer.

It's one of the most important life lessons to learn and yet hardly ever taught, including in the Torah world. No one ever really tells us that our entire life can come down to a single decision—and what that decision might be. And if we don't know what it might be, we can't really prepare for it and be ready to make it when that very fleeting yet critical moment arrives… even with some warning.

That is when many finally realize that in some cases, what you DON'T know CAN hurt you, especially when the gevuros realize that THEIR end is near.

THEY NEVER REALLY tell us about the moment of moments. Life for most people is just an endless series of have-to-make decisions, with the hope that they leave us in a good place. When we're old enough to understand it, someone should tell us that all of life can and probably will come down to a single monumental decision.

We should also be told not to expect much fanfare when that decision is made. Some of the most earth-shattering decisions have been made alone and in quiet. Even the person himself might not be aware he is making it at the time, not until he sees the amazing things it leads to.

In fact such moments very often just sneak up. We don't see them coming and barely ever see them leave. It is more like a hit-and-run incident, leaving behind some kind of intellectual or emotional impression that alters the way we think and live from that point onward.

Here's something else to consider. Such moments often come disguised in our own ignorance. This means that we lack information—perhaps about an opportunity of life in general—so that when the moment presents itself to us, we don't sufficiently appreciate what is at stake if we make one choice or the other. We may not notice until years later and sometimes not until after death.

Until Hitler, ysv"z, came to power and had the kind of support necessary to start capturing Jews, the average Jew made mostly local decisions. These are the everyday decisions we make just to get through a week. Rarely do they involve deciding to uproot an entire family to a safer place.

When word went out that the Nazis were rounding up Jews and killing them, the local decisions started becoming secondary as more global decisions made their way into everyday life. Future safety became a key issue, and discussions began to ensue about when you just pick up and leave everything behind, if you do at all.

For many there might have been a single moment when they had to decide to go in one direction or another and live forever with the consequences. At that time hardly anyone could imagine Hitler making good on his threats to such a degree. Had they realized otherwise, undoubtedly they would have picked up their families and left, knowing that staying behind was certain suicide.

Not only that, but there were moments when decisions were being made, individually and collectively, that might have led to the divine decree of shmad.[1] Jews who were exiled from Spain in 1492 later cited some mistaken community decisions that may have led to their fall from grace and expulsion from a once very hospitable Spain.

They say the Chofetz Chaim, who died in 1933, used to pound his table at seudas shlishis while crying out, "Millions are going to die, and no one is doing anything about it." Though lucid until his dying day, no one seems to have understood what he meant, or what to do about it. In the year he died Adolf Hitler, ysv"z, quite remarkably became Chancellor of Germany.

By 1942 we knew what the Chofetz Chaim had meant. We may never know how he came to know what he did, or why he couldn't be more specific in his calls for action, but it is clear that he sensed something on the scale of the Holocaust while the rest of the world, the Jewish world included, went about business

---

[1] Destruction; extreme oppression of Jews.

as usual.

Kristallnacht, which after the war was considered to be the beginning of the Holocaust, did not seem that way before the war. Yes, it was terrible and frightening, but who knew how far the Nazis would go at that point? Who was scared enough at that time to run for his life no matter what possessions he could not take with him? The fear didn't come until well after it was too late to do anything about it.

Maybe it's just the way it has to be. The Talmud speaks about levels of Divine Providence that are beyond our level of comprehension, especially when the worst of events occur at the best of times.[2] Kabbalah speaks about something similar called alillus, when God seems to use a pretext to carry out something bad He intended to do anyhow.[3]

It's all for the good. We know that. We declare that. And we've even seen many times how that is true well after the bad has occurred. Everything God does He does for our good,[4] and even though He acts out of anger, that is all He does—act. He doesn't lose His temper or EVER act recklessly, as we humans do. He never does anything that He has to regret later on. It's all planned, calculated, and for the good of mankind.

---

[2] Brochos 10a; Menachos 29b.

[3] Drushei Olam HaTohu, Chelek 2, Drush 4, Anaf 18, Siman 3.

[4] Brochos 61b.

Sometimes things go right despite our best efforts to make them go wrong. And sometimes things go wrong despite our best efforts to make them go right. History is much bigger than our personal life and incorporates all that has happened and all that has to happen. We don't even know what the rest of the same day will bring, so how can we possibly understand history on such a profound, DIVINE level?

Maybe the Jews were destined to get stuck in Spain and lose the opportunity to leave on their own terms. Perhaps the Jews of Europe never had a chance to leave en masse, even over a longer period of time. And perhaps the opportunity doesn't really exist for Diaspora Jews to make their move before the end of exile comes crashing down on them, God forbid, if it even does.

Perhaps. But paraphrasing what Yeshayahu told the righteous Chizkiah and would-be Moshiach, "What business do you have with the mysteries of God?[5] Your only responsibility is to do your part to know and carry out what God asks of you. Let HIM take care of the rest, including the results of your efforts to make things right."

But here's something that many people tend to forget: A person can intend good to happen and fail to get the intended result. Likewise, a person can in-

---

[5] Brochos 10a.

tend bad to happen and also have his plan fail. As the Talmud says, success and failure in this world depend on more than the intention of the person trying for the former and avoiding the latter.[6] Divine justice includes ALL the players pulled into a situation.

However, the person whose intention was good but failed for reasons beyond his control is credited with success nonetheless.[7] He did his part and was thwarted only because of other components of history that went beyond his own personal role in it. So why should he lose out?

On the contrary, a person whose intention was to do bad but failed at his plan should not think that he is off the hook as far as God is concerned. On the contrary, he remains quite on the hook, and will have to answer for his evil or just careless intention later on. Since he would have succeeded had not heaven intervened on behalf of the intended victim, from heaven's point of view it's as if he did succeed.

If people could only understand the value of their intentions to do good and the waste incurred by not caring enough about some particular situation that God DOES care about! The moment of moments may seem to fizzle and go out for us, but not for God. He just delays the result to a more appropriate time, when

----

[6] Brochos 33b.
[7] Brochos 6a.

it will have the best effect.

That's what it means when it says that God gives merit to those worthy of it and arranges for bad to happen through those who are not. The merit that made people worthy was making the right choice at the right time; neglecting that makes people unworthy.

Pinchas, grandson of Aharon HaKohen, is one of the best examples of this. When a Jewish prince took a Midianite princess against Torah law, a deadly plague ensued. It only stopped when Pinchas acted and avenged God, killing the sinners and becoming a kohen as a reward.[8]

The Talmud says that the rest of the nation was paralyzed. People didn't know how to respond, and Moshe Rabbeinu was held back from responding to give Pinchas a chance to leave his mark on Jewish history.

The question is why. Why was Pinchas singled out from the rest of the nation to do this historic act of zealousness and reap all the reward of doing so?

The answer is that at some time in his life Pinchas decided to live a life of zealousness. It may not have resulted in extreme behavior, at least extreme enough to catch the attention of others. Rather when he learned Torah and performed mitzvos, he did them with zeal, with a love of God and His Torah. He had

---

8 Bamidbar 25:1.

always been the zealot he was later proclaimed to be during the Midianite fiasco. That's just when God put him on the national stage to do his—and God's—thing.

How many in our generation have prepared like this for the Final Redemption? How many rabbis have been using their pulpits or stenders to address living in exile, and how to make sure that when the redemption started to reveal itself, their congregations would be ready to heed its call? Redemption and Eretz Yisroel have not been part of the curriculum for most, so many lack the intellectual tools to recognize when the time for them comes.

This is in spite of Jewish history, which has practically been one long ongoing tragic saga of being stuck in exile and losing the chance to escape it. We act as if the past is securely in the past, and can't return in the future, even though it has done so many times already, albeit with different nuances.

The Romans became the Crusaders, who became the Cossacks, who became the Nazis, etc. They had different clothing but they were all antisemites bent on destroying Jews or making them suffer. There is no reason to assume that there is not another group waiting to receive the baton of hatred and continue with the mission.

But there is good reason to assume that, just as in the past, many won't see it coming. Well, they'll see it coming all right, but they won't believe it is coming. They will hope that it will not go the same way it has gone in the past, and will gamble that life will get better, not worse. And when it doesn't—AGAIN—they will AGAIN wonder why they didn't learn from the past and save themselves and their families from what followed.

Again.

IT HAPPENS SO often, from zero to 90 in under two seconds. Peace of mind—gone, just like that. We see something or hear something that flicks some kind of switch, and our emotions are off and running. It can take an entire hour or more before we catch up to them and wonder how we got sucked into an emotional vacuum cleaner like dust into a real one.

With our loss of peace of mind, of course, our perspective goes as well. In the calm before the storm we knew that God runs the world and that no one else has power other than Him. We understood that He controls history and everyone else is just a pawn in HIS plan. We were believers.

But once that switch is flicked, it's a different story. We get angry at PEOPLE as if they have power to do wrong…AGAINST the will of God. We lose our religious perspective, and start seeing evil people all over the place.

It doesn't mean that evil people aren't evil. Very often they are. But we're about decision-making, and we're supposed to make CLEAR-HEADED decisions as much as possible. Heated-up emotions have never brought much in the way of rational thought to the decision-making table.

Sometimes that isn't such a bad thing. For instance, it can make people more generous. Someone may have planned to give $100 to charity, but after being moved almost to tears by the person asking, he instead wrote a check for $500—at least $200 more than he had available to give.

God doesn't mind that nearly as much as the opposite. "I was planning to help out," someone might say, "but when I saw THAT guy was involved, I felt anger surge inside me and I thought, 'I'm out of here!'" A worthy cause has to suffer because of a personal grudge?

In the first case not only will God appreciate generosity, but He'll pay it back, and then some. In the latter case God will come collecting, often forcing the gift-to-be-but-never-was out of the person in a far less meaningful way. The money he didn't give will go to some ridiculous repair, or the time will be wasted on some menial task, both of which cost something personally but neither of which provide any reward in the World-to-Come.

Part of being a good team player is knowing where you fit in, and doing your job well. Emotions are essential for being a good human being and having an enjoyable and meaningful life. The brain can tell us when and where to connect, but the emotions are what do the connecting and allow us to feel alive and well.

Emotions aren't rational, however. They're, well, emotional, and they seem to want a BIG say regarding anything dear to their hearts. And being emotional, they tend to be VERY loud…VERY bossy…and VERY distracting. When they get excited, they tend to steal the show, possessing us until we don't even recognize ourself anymore. Or at least the way we prefer to be recognized.

Passion is a great thing and a wonderful source of inspiration…when used in a moment that needs inspiration. But just as you wouldn't wear a tuxedo to a funeral, you don't wear your emotions to a moment that requires rational thinking.

How MANY, just HOW many lives have been lost because of uncalculated over-reaction? How much DAMAGE has resulted because people have put their emotions before their minds? Staggering amounts, and all because people weren't ready for the moment that ended up being a moment of moments.

But how do we do it? How do we rise above it all, especially when we truly have to, when the moment calls for it? What mechanisms are there for us to employ, regardless of our many different givens, like soul nature, family upbringing, education, friends, and other outside influences?

Truth Above All

"Do you solemnly swear to tell the truth, the whole truth, and nothing but the truth, so help you God, under pain and penalty of perjury?" This is the oath a witness usually has to take before presenting testimony in a secular court of law, with perhaps slight variations from society to society.

Question: Why is it even necessary?

Answer: People lie.

Even honest people. Even God has changed the truth on occasion to protect the innocent.[1] Human beings certainly lie, especially to protect the guilty when they themselves are guilty.

Sometimes the lie is only between the person and God, and no one else seems to lose out because of it. Other times the lie has catastrophic consequences for many people, maybe even large parts of

---

[1] Rashi, Bereishis 18:13. This is not an option for humans, however. Even slightly changing the truth should be an extremely rare occurrence—perhaps for the sake of shalom bayis, to save a fellow Jew from an enemy, or to protect a spouse with a severe heart condition—never to save one's own neck.

the world. We lie to protect what we cherish most when we think the truth endangers it.

The problem is that we humans have memories, and I am not talking about the memory we use to recall information. I'm talking about the kind of memory we use to create habits, both good and bad. If we do something often enough, it becomes our pattern in life. If we avoid the truth often enough, we can end up doing it almost automatically, even when we'd rather have admitted the truth.

If we look at life a certain way, life will appear to us that way, even if that particular way of looking at it is wrong. Your best friends will likely have a common way of viewing life, but just talk to a neighbor and see how someone else has fit reality into his own point of view. It can get really wild sometimes, and make you wonder how such people manage to function in the world.

Why should people even care about the truth? Obviously if they were born to believe in it, it is not a question. It is the way they were trained to live life, and hopefully the truth they were trained to pursue is the accurate one.

But what about the others?

If people do not believe in God, or at least in Torah, then there really isn't a good answer FROM THEIR PERSPECTIVE. First of all, from THEIR perspective there really isn't any truth, just a lot of personal opinions, as mentioned previously. Why shouldn't they lie when it seems to be in their best interests?

From a Torah perspective, their best interests are to pursue truth and live according to it. This is what the Torah is telling us when it says that man was made in the image of God.[2] Every human being—even pathological liars—are cut from the same cloth of truth, making it an essential part of being human. Hardwired for truth, we erode our own peace of mind when we fudge it.

And when the truth hurts, it does so for a reason. Falsehood bends reality. Truth bends it back. If you leave an improperly healed leg alone, it will only become worse in the future. Instead it can be broken again and then set right, so that it will be less problematic in the future.

You can't always walk into a situation—especially with other people and even more so when there is controversy—and call out, "Okay, what's the TRUTH here?" But you can think it and let it be your guiding principle. You can make truth the glasses through which you view every situation, simple or complicated, trivial or serious. You can make the truth matter to you above all else, and it will serve you well throughout life.

Know the Goal

Being afraid of making a mistake is not the same

---

[2] Bereishis 1:26.

as being a perfectionist. Perfectionists can see mistakes even where they don't exist, as they pursue what they believe is perfection. A person who fears error can accept less than perfect results as long as the intended goal is accomplished.

Part of the problem is that people don't know what the goal is. For some it is enough to live and die as Torah Jews. After death there will be a divine tribunal to decide their fate henceforth, which hopefully will be the World-to-Come, without their having to spend any or much time in Gehinom.

They know that there are things called Geulah Shlaimah, complete redemption; Yemos HaMoshiach, Days of Moshiach; and Techiyas HaMeisim, resurrection of the dead. But when, what, how? These considerations are not on their hashkofic[3] radar. For such people if Moshiach doesn't come in their lifetimes, it is no failure. If they don't witness the redemption, well, neither will many others.

But it IS a failure, and one for which they will bear some responsibility if they didn't do THEIR best to make it happen. It is supposed to be the goal of all Jews to have the world recognize God as their God and King too. As the PROPHET said, and WE repeat thrice daily, "God will be King over the entire land, and

---

[3] Torah philosophical outlook.

on that day God will be One, and His Name, One."[4]

That is the Jewish goal.

That is our mission statement.

That is supposed to be our focus.

In computer language, it is our background task. We go to shul daily and try to learn some Torah while also earning a parnassah to support our family. We have children to educate and eventually marry off. We have to achieve and maintain shalom bayis, a good marital relationship. All this alone is enough to exhaust us by the end of the day.

But day after day, the Shechinah—Divine Presence—remains in exile. The holy Temple does not stand in its holy place, but in its stead is a foreign house of worship, surrounded by others. Most Jews do not live by Torah, those who do are not always consistent, and those who don't are extremely secular. History is clearly not on track.

This has to change, and it WILL change. The only questions are how and when. God certainly asks those questions, even though He already knows the answers. Do we? If we're at all truthful, we'll be honest about our assessment, and it should temper the way we define personal success.

Life from a historical point of view can't help but elevate people above everyday mundane reality.

---

[4] Zechariah 14:9.

Personal Perception

It is always interesting to watch yourself in a video when you didn't know you were being filmed. You get to see yourself more objectively—and it is often insightful.

People have images of who they want to be and how close they are to being it. But they can be wrong and don't always take the word of others to tell them that. It's harder to fool yourself when you see something with your own eyes.

Self-honesty is key, but it also helps to have a well-defined mental description of who you think you should be, especially in heated situations. It doesn't hurt either to practice the part, perhaps in front of a mirror. It imprints the image and actions into the brain during calmer moments, so that when you act out of character during excited moments, you can sense it better and make the necessary changes before getting swallowed up by the moment.

Be Mindful, Not Arrogant

There are almost 8 billion people in the world. It would be nice if we were all equal and treated each other equally. As it says, "Don't do to others what you would not want done to you."[5] Just as you want people to be patient with you as you get up to speed, so

---

5 Shabbos 31a.

too should you be patient with others if they are not keeping pace with you. Patience is not only a virtue, but one of the most important of all virtues.

Furthermore, it is human nature for people to be self-protective and to want to get ahead in life, sometimes even at the expense of others. We may not like it but it is reality. It is also a function of many things that people may have missed out on in life, that left them injured or just blindsided. Or they could simply be having a bad day, and you are unfortunately getting the brunt of it.

A person has to constantly be mindful that, as similar as people are, they are also quite different. Some are moodier than others, some less moody. Some are more high strung than others, some less. It might even help from the outset to remind ourself of this before interacting with new people or people who have a reputation for being moody or high strung.

Mindful—but not arrogant. No one has the right to wrong another, but a lot of people do not even realize they are doing it. Nevertheless, arrogance has never served people well. If anything, it only worsens a situation and adds to the frustration of the moment. Arrogance is usually a lose-lose situation.

Trust in God

Ultimately there really is only one authentic way to rise above it all, and that is with bitachon—trust in

God. People cannot lift a finger against anyone without God's permission, and they can't do either good or bad to someone else or even to themselves if God is not on board.

All life is just one long, ongoing test. It is a test to show us who we are and what we're capable of achieving. We may not see life as a test or in key moments remember that it is one, but that is what it always is, no matter if we're by ourself or in a large crowd.

But we see people. We hear people. It is people who seem to make us happy or miserable. Even though we all are real people with real free will, we still always work on behalf of God, wittingly or unwittingly, especially when we interact with others. It is both the most important thing to remember and the easiest to forget.

Bitachon is not something you can just turn on or off. It's like a muscle: it has to be developed, strengthened, and maintained. That means working on it during the quiet, non-bitachon moments, when we can make a point of driving the underlying concepts of trust and God into our mind and imagining how to apply them to different situations.

To stay above a situation is much easier than it is to rise above it after it begins. A ba'al bitachon, someone who works on mastering the trait, will be able to be tested with confrontation and not capitulate to it. Bitachon fortifies us against attack of any sort, providing much desired peace of mind as a result.

And peace of mind is the most important back-drop of all when it comes to trying to respond correctly to a moment of moments.

It's Not Funny

ten

BUT MAYBE IT should be. It certainly seems as if something magical happens to our perspective on life after a good laugh. It's as if we can get so wound up in life that we lose focus and clarity. A good laugh seems to unwind us and bring us back down, or up as the case may be, to reality.

They say that laughter is the best medicine. A good, hearty laugh relieves physical tension and stress, leaving muscles relaxed for up to 45 minutes afterward. It also boosts the immune system, decreases stress hormones, and increases immune cells and infection-fighting antibodies,[1] thus improving resis-

---

[1] https://www.helpguide.org/articles/mental-health/laughter-is-the-best-medicine.htm

tance to disease.

Laughter reduces pain and allows us to tolerate discomfort. It increases job performance, connects people emotionally, and improves the flow of oxygen to the heart and brain. Laughter has even been proven to help patients to fight cancer.[2]

The same benefits apply to making good decisions. It's interesting that the Hebrew word for clear thinking is tzalul, a word used to refer to a clear liquid. When anything unnecessary is added to water, like sediment for example, the water ceases to be clear. When you add extraneous thoughts to a decision, it too ceases to be clear.

Just as with respect to water, you can add something to your thinking to make a solution better, not worse. How about worry? Does worry make you think more clearly or less clearly, especially if the worry is about the topic at hand?

It doesn't matter:

Worrying is feeling uneasy or being overly concerned about a situation or problem. With excessive worrying, your mind and body go into overdrive as you constantly focus on "what might happen." In the midst of excessive worrying, you

---

[2] https://www.helpguide.org/articles/mental-health/laughter-is-the-best-medicine.htm

may suffer from high anxiety—even panic—during waking hours. Many chronic worriers tell of feeling a sense of impending doom or unrealistic fears that only increase their worries. Ultra-sensitive to their environment and to the criticism of others, excessive worriers may see anything—and anyone—as a potential threat.[3]

But that's just with respect to excessive worry, you say. Everyone worries a little, and it doesn't really affect the way he deals with his decision-making.

Au contraire.

Have you ever thought you were focused on a discussion with someone until he suddenly asks, "Are you with me?" At that moment you realize that you weren't. And when you wonder where you were, you can't even say for sure, at least not without taking time to retrace your mental steps.

Do you ever feel a sense of dread without being sure why? Nothing around you seems worrisome, yet you feel anxious. Sometimes you can figure it out and other times it remains such a mystery that you wonder if it is some kind of sixth sense of impending danger!

According to the Talmud, there is such a thing,[4]

------

[3] https://www.webmd.com/balance/guide/how-worrying-affects-your-body#1

[4] Megillah 3a.

but chances are that most of us aren't in touch with it. More than likely you are worried on a subconscious level, and the brain is just trying to multitask without your permission.

The trouble is that the brain doesn't have unlimited resources—at least ones that WE can access without some mystical skill. We can try to do two things at once, but neither will be at optimum level. It's like a pie: the more you share, the less you get, and much of the time we don't even know we're sharing brain energy.

God has wired us so that our autonomic reflexes don't interfere with our conscious level of living. But add a negative emotion to the pot and it will definitely interfere, even to the point of taking over conscious life and causing self-destruction.

So people may think they are being clear-headed when confronting a moment, but they can easily be distracted, at least partially. Accidents, many of them tragic and deadly, happen because people assumed they were in full control of their mental faculties—but they weren't.

Until we master meditation, we don't even really know how much control it's possible to have over our mind. Until we struggle to master it, we have no idea how much we capitulate to the whims of the brain on a daily basis, allowing it to go just about anywhere it wants, whenever it wants to.

Mindfulness is a term coined to make money. Just kidding. The term was created to (1) tell people they are not focused enough in each moment and (2) how to change that. The moment one sentence of mine ends differently from what you expected, you become a bit more mindful of the next sentence.

There are many different ways to achieve mindfulness, some of which work better for some people and some for others. Although fear can make a person quite mindful, the resulting worry of impending danger or other negative emotions can quickly undo its focus-causing benefit.

That's why it is suggested that speakers begin sessions with a good joke. If they begin with fear, they may lose out on attention as people try to recover from negative excitement and overcome adverse feelings about the cause of it.

A good joke, on the other hand, makes friends. But it does more than loosen up a crowd or work an audience. It draws people together. It gets their attention. It focuses them, making them better receptors for information. Used wisely, humor can move mountains. It can certainly change someone's mood on a dime.

Unless of course the sad or depressed person chooses to remain that way. Sometimes THAT might be necessary, for example while mourning the loss of a loved one. To use humor at moments like that will undoubtedly have the reverse effect. Not because something isn't funny, but rather because people don't want to know about it.

Humor can be found in just about any situation if you know where and how to look. That's one of the funny things about humor. It can be found even in situations that on the surface don't seem to be very funny.

Take heaven, for example. Well, you can't actually TAKE heaven, but you can use it as an example. It seems like such a serious place. I mean, when you think of God, you think of SERIOUS. Do they even laugh in heaven? Do angels know what laughter is? Do the souls of people who laughed down here remember the fun of it when they are up there? On the other hand, if humor weren't so godly, would God have made it such an integral part of good health?

Interesting questions lacking interesting answers, but sometimes things happen down here that make it seem as if they do have a sense of humor up there. Or at least that some of the angels do. It was God Who named one of the forefathers Yitzchak—he will laugh.[5]

Who will laugh? Rashi says this refers to people who hear about the miraculous birth and wonder how a 90-year-old barren woman returned to her youthfulness and gave birth to a son from a man who was 100 years young! And the really funny thing is that of all the forefathers Yitzchak seems to be the most serious. Un-

---

[5] Bereishis 17:19.

til, that is, you read this:

> [God] said to Yitzchak: "Your children have sinned against Me."
>
> Yitzchak said before Him: "Master of the Universe, are they my children and not Your children? At Sinai, when they first said before You, 'We will do' and then 'We will listen,' didn't You call them 'My son, My firstborn son Yisroel'? Now that they have sinned, are they my children and not Your children? And furthermore, how much did they actually sin? How long is a person's life? Seventy years. Subtract [the first] 20 [years of life for which a person is] not punished [regarding heavenly matters, and] 50 [years] remain. Subtract 25 [years] of nights, [and] 25 [years] remain. Subtract [another] twelve-and-a-half [years during which] one prays and eats and [uses] the bathroom, and twelve-and-a-half [years] remain. If You [can] endure them all [and forgive the sins committed during those years], excellent. If not, half [the sins are] on me [to bear] and half on You. And if You say [that] all of them [are] on me, I sacrificed myself before You [and You should forgive them due to my merit]!" (Shabbos 89a)

What a remarkable conversation between a human being and the Creator of the Universe. "Twelve-

and-a-half years in the bathroom"…when you're talking to the Creator…and the fate of the Jewish people
is in the balance? I guess if you're Yitzchak, you can
bargain like that.

Then there is this insightful discussion from the
Talmud:

> On that day [when they discussed this matter],
> Rebi Eliezer responded to all [possible] answers in
> the world [to support his opinion], but they [the
> rabbis] did not accept [the explanations] from
> him.
>
> [After failing to convince the rabbis logically,
> Rebi Eliezer] said to them: "If the law is like my
> opinion, this carob tree will prove it."
>
> The carob tree was uprooted from its place 100
> amos, and some say 400 amos,[6] but [the rabbis]
> said to him: "One does not cite proof from the
> carob tree!"
>
> [Rebi Eliezer] then said to them: "If the law is
> like my opinion, the stream will prove it."
>
> [The water in] the stream turned backward [and
> began flowing in the opposite direction]. They
> said to him: "One does not cite proof from a
> stream!"
>
> [Rebi Eliezer] then said to them: "If [the] law is

---

[6] About 200 and 800 feet, respectively.

according to my [opinion], then the walls of the study hall will prove it."

The walls of the study hall leaned [inward and began] to fall. Rabbi Yehoshua scolded [the walls] and said to them: "If Torah scholars are contending with each other in [matters of] law, how can you interfere?"

They did not fall because of the deference due Rabbi Yehoshua, but they did not straighten because of the deference due Rabbi Eliezer, and they still remain leaning. [Rebi Eliezer] then said to them: "If the law is like my opinion, heaven will prove it."

A divine voice emerged from heaven and said: "Why are you differing with Rebi Eliezer, since the law is in accordance with his opinion in every place that he has an opinion?"

Rabbi Yehoshua stood on his feet and said: "[It is written:] 'It is not in heaven!' [Devarim 30:12]"

What [did he mean by] "It is not in heaven"? Rebi Yirmiyah says: "[Since] the Torah was already given at Mount Sinai, we do not regard a divine voice, as You already said at Mount Sinai in the Torah: 'Go after a majority' [Shemos 23:2]. [Since the majority of rabbis disagreed with Rabbi Eliezer's opinion, the law is not ruled in accordance with his opinion.]

[Later] Rebi Nosan met Eliyahu and asked him:

"What did the Holy One, Blessed Is He, do at that time [when Rebi Yehoshua made his declaration]?"

[Eliyahu] answered: "He smiled and said: 'My children have triumphed over Me! My children have triumphed over Me!'" (Bava Metzia 59b)

One thing is for sure: no other religion has ever recorded a discussion like this that has God, in the end, admit defeat and actually laugh about it. Some would consider it heresy!

And not only do we like to laugh, but we like to make others laugh perhaps even more. There is something very rewarding about making others laugh, especially when they say things like "You are so funny." One person commented how the thrill of his day was just making his elderly parent crack a smile or laugh out loud. It lifted his own spirits.

What actually happens when we laugh?

Laughing hysterically releases endorphins, which makes you happy…Just the physical act of laughing—as in the muscular movements involved in producing the sound—prompts an increase in endorphins. One study experimented with the electrical activity that occurs when we laugh. "About four-tenths of a second after we hear the punch line of a joke—even before we laugh—a wave of electricity sweeps through the cortex," reports Peter Derks, a professor of psychology at the College of William and Mary. "What Derks finds most significant about this wave is that it carpets our entire cerebral cortex, rather than just one region," writes Peter Doskoch.[7] "So all or most of our higher brain may play a role in laughter, perhaps with the left hemisphere working on the joke's verbal content while the analytic right hemisphere attempts to figure out the incongruity that lies at the heart of much humor."[8]

Which brings us back to the main point. It's a simple point. The more of the brain we involve in a situation, the more of ourself is also there. Physically we can't be in two places at one time. But mentally? We CAN be all over the place at the same moment, limiting the brain's ability to fully process what is happening at the time.

It is interesting how humor in particular has the ability to pull us together mentally to better experience a moment of time. This explains why we like humor so much and feel so much more alive when we

---

[7] https://www.psychologytoday.com/articles/199607/happily-ever-laughter.

[8] https://thethirty.whowhatwear.com/what-happens-to-your-brain-when-you-laugh

experience it. Who wouldn't pay to feel better about life, to feel that life is good, even when it seems as if it really isn't?

It will probably not seem appropriate to others if, at their time of crisis—which requires quick decision-making—you do a stand-up comedy act. People certainly don't appreciate your pointing out something humorous in what they find extremely serious. But people report that they have often come up with good solutions to problems when they themselves have used humor.

At the very least, a humorous approach can eliminate the sense of doom and gloom that often overshadows a crisis. It creates instead a sense that all is not lost, which helps the brain to focus and find a solution. If people believe there is a way out, they are more likely to find it.

That is why, in my opinion, a classic example of in-a-crisis-humor is this one:

> Pharaoh drew near, and the Children of Israel lifted up their eyes, and behold! The Egyptians were advancing after them. They were very frightened, and the Children of Israel cried out to God. They said to Moshe, "Is it because there are no graves in Egypt that you have taken us to die in the desert?" (Shemos 14:10-11)

There the Jewish people were, between a hard rock and a wall. In this case the wall was the Reed Sea in front of them; the hard rock was the advancing and ruthless Egyptian army behind them. The situation was bleak, even hopeless, so the Jewish people were… were sarcastic?

"Hey, Moshe," you can almost hear them saying, "Great situation you and God brought us into. Deadly sea in front of us, deadly army behind us! Tell us, did you do this because there weren't enough places to bury all of us back in Egypt so you took us out of there to bury us here in the desert instead?"

One of the great things about sarcasm is that it isn't cynicism, the trait of Amalek. Cynicism means a person has already given up and is only working on making do with the situation as is. You never go to a cynic when you want to solve a problem, but only when you want to mourn it.

Sarcasm can have an element of hostility, especially among people who don't share trust, but it also boosts creativity and might inspire something like this: "Hmm, this is weird. We would have thought that something better should have occurred here, but for some ironic reason, it didn't. Is there any way to fix this?"

It is interesting that the Torah even recorded the statement of the people at the sea. It would seem that more important than telling us what happened at that crucial moment, the Torah is showing us how to react to it…with a little humor. After all, it does say about the End-of-Days:

> A song of ascents. When God returns the returnees to Tzion, we will be like dreamers. Then our mouths will be filled with LAUGHTER… (Tehillim 126:1-2)

Laughter? Why laughter? Because that is when we'll finally be able to look back on all history and see the humor in it. We'll be able to see it all from God's perspective, and how everything God did really was for the good.[9] What it actually was and what we thought at the time will be so very different that it will seem, well, humorous. Apparently the End-of-Days will be funny.

Let's face it. One reason so many people miss their moments of moments is because they were distracted. It wasn't due to their being busy laughing at life because, had they done that, they would have experienced more and gained greater perspectives on truth. Laughter would have left them better prepared for such moments, as well as more focused to deal with them.

Distraction is one of the oldest tricks in the book

---

[9] Brochos 61b.

for the yetzer hara. It makes us take life and ourself too seriously, which in the end prevents us from taking both seriously enough. Uptight people often run to distractions to ease their burdens. In doing so, they end up some place other than where they be—a place they definitely should not be.

People who can find the humor in life tend to be in balance with it. They're not mocking life. They're noting where life mocks itself, and they can therefore share a laugh with it. They can be healthier for it too, physically, mentally, spiritually, and most important of all, they can be ready to appropriately deal with the moment of moments when it comes their way.

I ONCE LED a group of young couples on a leadership mission to Israel. Since I went to Israel ahead of them, I purchased a separate ticket. At the end of the mission I planned to fly back at the same time as the group, albeit on a different plane..

The entire trip went like clockwork. After a successful and impactful two weeks we were standing in line in Jerusalem at early check-in, a service that El Al provided in those days which made it easier for everyone at the airport at the time of the flight.

When it was my turn to check in, I approached the counter as others had done before me and nonchalantly handed my ticket and passport to the attendant. Assuming everything was fine, I just kept talking to the people behind me as she began the process of preparing my boarding pass.

Then came the "good" news.

"Sir, your flight left this morning at 1 a.m."

It took a minute for my brain to switch modes and understand what she was saying, so she pointed to my ticket and said. "Your flight was for 1 a.m. this morning."

I froze in confusion and panic.

She told me that it was not an uncommon mistake with these flights. Since the flight is after midnight, it is already the next day. Some people mistakenly assume that the flight is in the afternoon, rather than the wee hours of morning, so they miss their flight.

As I was sleeping soundly at my hotel, my plane loaded its passengers and baggage. It took off and was well over the Atlantic by the time I had finished praying and eating breakfast, with my seat on the plane likely vacant. By the time I got to my FIRST destination, early check-in, the plane was approaching its FINAL destination, 6,000 miles away! Talk about missing the boat.

It didn't take long for the consequences of my error to sink in. I would have to leave later. Ouch. And I would have to pay for an additional ticket, which had not been part of the budget, neither the trip's nor mine. DOUBLE OUCH!

Fortunately God, in His infinite mercy, had arranged that my attendant was not only pleasant but sympathetic. Even without crying—probably the shock on my face was enough—she started checking around on her computer. There was room on the plane that my students were taking…and El Al would not charge me for a new ticket.

THANK GOD.

HUGE SIGH OF RELIEF.

Even though I came out on top, thank God, the lesson was not lost on me. When something like that happens, I automatically try to extract some kind of life lesson from it. Everything is Hashgochah Pratis—Divine Providence—so by definition everything is meant to teach us something about life.

In the context of this book that lesson is clear. I had missed my moment without even knowing it, assuming the whole time that it was still ahead of me. And the ironic thing is that the information I needed in order to seize it in its time was right there in front of me—a.m., not p.m.

How many people will get to check-in after they have left this world, assuming that everything is in order, and find out otherwise? How many people go to the grave thinking that the path they followed was the best one for them, only to discover it wasn't even close? What will souls say when they meet their Maker after spending an entire life claiming He didn't exist?

Probably everyone has a moment of truth. That's when we experience something that catches our attention and makes us think and wonder about life on some level. It can be so subtle that we are barely conscious of it, but it impacts us nonetheless. It's at that point we get to choose to go either right or left…for the rest of our life.

After it passes, we may never get a second chance. And as times moves on, that moment gets buried in the past, forgotten, no longer recognizable in any way. When we ask ourself, if we do ask ourself, "How did I get this way?" we really have no clue.

Then we get to heaven and we are asked the same question. We have to say, "I have no idea." But the questioners know. They take out the reel and start playing it, reversing all the way back to that one little, unremarkable, critical, potentially life-altering moment. "There," they say. "Right there. That's the moment that could have made your life so much better, as well as your time now in eternity."

As we study the moment, we can't recall it. It is clearly there because we can see it now, so it surely must have happened, but we just can't recall it, or only vaguely recall it. "THAT moment?" our soul says incredulously. "THAT was my moment…"

"Of moments," they say. "It was YOUR moment of moments…and you missed it…COMPLETELY!"

"But how is that fair?" we argue in defense. "I had no idea that anything special was going on at the time!"

"Only those who prepare on Erev Shabbos eat on Shabbos,"[1] they say.

"Huh?"

"It's a saying in the Talmud. You can't cook on Shabbos so, if you want to eat cooked food, you have to prepare before Shabbos. But it is also an analogy for ALL of life. If you want to be ready to take full advantage of your personal moment of moments, you have to prepare for it."

"Prepare? How?"

"You could have started by asking some simple and rather obvious questions: What is the purpose of life? How do we know? Introspecting on those two questions would have set you off in the right direction, and then heaven would have helped you find your way. It always does for people who sincerely ask such questions."[2]

As we contemplate the criticism and try to recall whether we ever asked ourself such obvious questions, we are further told, "We find it quite amazing up here how many people don't even bother to think about this. Even if they do, many stop well short of finding a good source for their answer. People just make assumptions and drift. They mistake their success as either divine approval or a lack of need for it. Crazy, isn't

---

[1] Avodah Zarah 3a.

[2] Yoma 38b.

it?"
        Yeah, crazy. Isn't it?

THE FOLLOWING TITLES are all the books written over the years. Some books may no longer be in print, but many are still available in either PDF or Kindle formats. Visit the Thirtysix.org OnLine Bookstore, or Amazon for more information, or to order online.

The Unbroken Chain of Jewish Tradition, 1985
The Eternal Link, 1990
If Only I Were Wealthy, 1992
If Only I Understood Why, 1993
If Only I Could See the Forest, 1993
If Only I Could Stay, 1993
If Only Great Was Greater, 1993
The Y Factor, 1994
Life's A Thrill, 1994

No Atheists in a Foxhole, 1994
Changes that Last Forever, 1994
The Making of a Great Jewish Leader, 1994
Bereishis: A Beginning With No End, 1994
The Wonderful World of Thirtysix, 1995
Redemption to Redemption, 1997
The Big Picture, 1998
Perceptions, 1998
Not Just Another Scenario, 2001
At The Threshold, 2001
Anticipating Redemption, 2002
Sha'ar HaGilgulim, 2002
Hadran (Hebrew), 2004
Talking About The End of Days, 2005
Talking About Eretz Yisroel, 2005
The Physics of Kabbalah, 2006
Be Positive, 2007
Geulah b'Rachamim, 2007
God.calm, 2007
Just Passing Through, 2007
On The Same Page, 2007
The Equation of Life, 2007
No Such Victim, 2009
Survival in 10 Easy Steps, 2009
Not Just Another Scenario 2, 2011
All In Your Mind, 2011
The Light of Thirtysix, 2011
The Last Exile, 2011

Drowning in Pshat, 2012
Drown No More, 2012
Shas Man, 2013
The Mystery of Jewish History, 2013
Survival Guide For the End-of-Days, 2013
Deeper Perceptions, 2013
Chanukah Lite, 2015
The Hitchhiker's Guide to Armageddon, 2016
Purim Lite, 2016
Pesach Lite, 2016
The Torah Empowerment Seminar, 2016
Siman Tov (Hebrew), 2016
The Fabric of Reality, 2016
Addendum, 2016
Fundamentals of Reincarnation, 2017
Reincarnation Clarified, 2016
All About Energy, 2017
What Goes Around, 2017
The God Experience, 2017
What in Heaven, 2017
The God Experience, Part 2, 2017
The God Experience, Part 3, 2017
It's About Time, 2017
Need to Know, 2017
Perceptions, Volume 2, 2017
Once Revealed, Twice Concealed, 2017
The Art of Chayn, 2017
A Matter of Laugh or Death, 2018

Geulah b'Rachamim Program, V. 1, 2018
Geulah b'Rachamim Program, V. 2, 2018
Geulah b'Rachamim Program, V. 3, 2018
Point of Acceptance, 2018
See Ya, 2018
In Discussion: Bereishis, 2018
Reincarnation Again, 2018
A Separate Matter, 2018
In Discussion: Shemos, 2019
A Search for Self, 2019
A Search for Trust, 2019
In Discussion: Bamidbar, 2019
How It Might Play Out, 2019
In Discussion: Vayikra, 2019
Where Are My Emotions Now, 2019
In Discussion: Devarim, 2019
The Early Years, 2019
Oh, So Blind, 2019
Not So Bad? 2019
Sha'ar HaPesukim: Shemos, 2019
The Fix, 2020
Sha'ar HaPesukim: Bereishis, 2020
Preparing For Redemption, 2020
Mindfulness, Torah & Redemption, 2020

For more information, write to pinchasw@thirtysix.org,

thirtysix.org